D0435671

CAMBAT... LIBRARY

DATE DUE

[DEC] 4 1996		
APR O 4 1998		
APR. 2 2 1998		
NOV 1 3 2005		
DEC 1 3 2005		

YA $11.95 1-96
305.42   At issue: What is
ATI   sexual harassment
Copy 1

DEMCO

WHAT IS SEXUAL HARASSMENT?

Other Books in the At Issue Series:

WHAT IS SEXUAL HARASSMENT?

David Bender, *Publisher*
Bruno Leone, *Executive Editor*

Katie de Koster, *Managing Editor*
Scott Barbour, *Series Editor*

Karin L. Swisher, *Book Editor*

An Opposing Viewpoints Series®

Greenhaven Press, Inc.
San Diego, California

No part of this book may be reproduced or used in any form or by any means, electrical, mechanical, or otherwise, including, but not limited to, photocopy, recording, or any information storage and retrieval system, without prior written permission from the publisher.

Library of Congress Cataloging-in-Publication Data

At issue: What is sexual harassment? / book editor, Karin Swisher.
        p.   cm. — (At issue series) (An opposing viewpoints series)
    Includes bibliographical references and index.
    ISBN 1-56510-266-5 (pbk.) — ISBN 1-56510-299-1 (lib.).
    1. Sexual harassment. [1. Sexual harassment.] I. Swisher, Karin,
1966-   . II. Title: What is sexual harassment?. III. Series. IV. Series:
Opposing viewpoints series (Unnumbered)
HQ1237.A85   1995   94-28345
305.42—dc20   CIP
                                                               AC

YA

© 1995 by Greenhaven Press, Inc., PO Box 289009,
San Diego, CA 92198-9009

Printed in the U.S.A.

Every effort has been made to trace owners of copyrighted material.

Table of Contents

Introduction

Sexual harassment is a relatively new term for an age-old complaint. For example, Genesis 39 in the Bible tells of a woman who tried to force her husband's male servant, Joseph, to "lie with" her; when he refused, she retaliated by having him imprisoned for attempted rape. In the 1600s, one English couple had a long-running dispute about what kind of maid they should have. The wife refused to hire a pretty one and the husband refused to have any other kind. They compromised on a "liquourish" girl. When she was discovered drinking her employer's wine, the master forced her to submit to his advances or be sent to prison for theft.

Despite its long history, this type of behavior went unnamed until the mid-1970s, when the term "sexual harassment" was coined; and it did not become the subject of long, heated national debate until, during the 1991 confirmation hearings for his current position as U.S. Supreme Court justice, Clarence Thomas was accused by a former employee, law professor Anita Hill, of sexual harassment. While Hill's allegation ultimately did not derail Thomas's confirmation, the televised Senate hearings and other media coverage did help bring sexual harassment to the forefront of the nation's consciousness. According to Lynn Hecht Safran, an attorney for the National Organization for Women's Legal Defense and Education Fund, "The national debate sparked by Professor Hill's allegations has infused women with a new determination to have this issue taken seriously."

Feminist legal scholar Catharine MacKinnon notes that "the unnamed should not be taken for the nonexistent." But until sexual harassment was given a name in the 1970s, American society did not formulate public policies to define or prevent it. As the social response to sexual harassment increased, the definition of the term began to evolve, shaped primarily by the federal government and the court system.

Two social phenomena helped bring sexual harassment to the public's attention. First, women began to enter the workforce in increasing numbers. In 1959, there were 22 million women in the workplace. That number has steadily increased—by 1991 there were 57 million working women. A second influence was the movement for equal rights for women, a movement given added impetus by such developments as the birth control pill (which allowed women to control their own reproduction), the concomitant "sexual revolution" of the 1960s and 1970s (which encouraged openness about sexual matters and mutually satisfying relations between partners), and a proliferation of women's support and consciousness-raising groups. These contributed to a shift both in the way women and sexuality were viewed—for example, women were no longer automatically blamed for being raped—and in what women were willing to put up with. It was in this atmosphere that women began to realize that they had recourse against the unwanted advances of male coworkers and began to bring lawsuits against their harassers. According to Charles Clark, writing in the August 1991 *CQ Researcher,* "The 1970s ushered in an era of dramatic efforts to curb workplace discrimination of all forms."

The first federal law that would eventually make discrimination against women—including sexual harassment—illegal was the Civil Rights Act. Passed in 1964 by the Lyndon Johnson administration, the act bars discrimination in employment based on race, color, sex, religion, or national origin. Ironically, however, according to Lynne Eisaguirre, author of *Sexual Harassment,* when it was introduced the civil rights bill did not protect against discrimination based on sex. She reports:

> Discrimination based on gender is attached to the bill at the last moment, when conservative Southern opponents introduce an amendment prohibiting discrimination on the basis of sex; they assume that adding sexual equality is so preposterous that the amendment will scuttle the entire bill. . . . The Johnson administration wants the Civil Rights Act passed so badly that it decides not to oppose the amendment.

This almost accidental protection against discrimination laid the groundwork for the first sexual harassment cases brought during the mid-1970s.

Early efforts to use the Civil Rights Act to redress sexual harassment proved unsuccessful. According to sexual harassment consultant Susan Webb, in the first three cases, *Miller* v. *Bank of America, Corne* v. *Bausch & Lomb,* and *Barnes* v. *Train,* the courts interpreted "sexual harassment based on sex as a 'personal matter' between the two individuals, and not as action directed at or affecting groups of people," as was required to bring the Civil Rights Act into effect. In 1976, however, in *Williams* v. *Saxbe,* an employee claimed that her supervisor harassed her and then fired her after she refused to have sex with him. This time the judge found sexual harassment to be "based on sex" and within the meaning of Title VII of the Civil Rights Act, which prohibits discrimination based on sex and discrimination in the workplace. According to Webb, "This was a major and landmark decision in beginning to redress sexual harassment in the workplace."

In 1977, two of the first three cases (*Miller* and *Corne*), along with a third early case, *Tomkins* v. *Public Service Electric & Gas,* were appealed, and the appellate courts overturned the initial decisions. According to Eisaguirre, "All three appellate courts rule that a harassed woman has a right, under Title VII of the Civil Rights Act, to sue the corporate entity that employed her." *Tomkins* stated that the courts would no longer view harassment as a personal problem, but as sex discrimination; however, they would require the women bringing suit to show a clear relationship between the sexual harassment and termination, undesirable job assignments, or poor performance reviews.

The first claim of sexual harassment under Title IX of the 1972 Education Act Amendments, which prohibits discrimination based on sex by universities and other schools receiving federal funds, was filed in 1977. In *Alexander* v. *Yale,* a female student claimed that her professor offered her an A in a class in exchange for sex and told her she would get a C if she refused. A district court held that sexual harassment may constitute sex discrimination under Title IX. For the first time, legal definitions of sexual harassment could also be applied to academia.

Efforts to define sexual harassment in the court system were echoed in 1980 within the federal government. In November 1980, the Equal

Employment Opportunity Commission (EEOC), created by the Civil Rights Act and chaired by Eleanor Holmes Norton, issued a series of guidelines on sex discrimination. The EEOC guidelines stated:

> Harassment on the basis of sex is a violation of [the law]. Unwelcome sexual advances, requests for sexual favors and other verbal or physical conduct of a sexual nature constitute sexual harassment when:
>
> 1. submission to such conduct is made either explicitly or implicitly a term or condition of an individual's employment,
> 2. submission to or rejection of such conduct by an individual is used as the basis for employment decisions affecting such individual, or
> 3. such conduct has the purpose or effect of unreasonably interfering with an individual's work performance or creating an intimidating, hostile, or offensive work environment.

Numbers 1 and 2 of the guidelines constitute what is known as "quid pro quo" sexual harassment. Number 3 is more commonly known as "hostile environment" sexual harassment. The EEOC guidelines mark the first definition of sexual harassment to include hostile environment.

In the early 1980s, the hostile environment argument was successfully employed for the first time in *Brown* v. *City of Guthrie*. Even though the plaintiff could not show loss of tangible job benefits, she did establish that sexual harassment had created a hostile, offensive, and unbearable work environment. The court that decided the *Brown* case cited the EEOC Guidelines in the record.

In 1986, in *Meritor Savings Bank* v. *Vinson*, the United States Supreme Court ruled that sexual harassment on the job is illegal discrimination even if the victim suffers no economic loss. In its first ruling on sexual harassment, the Court included hostile environment sexual harassment in its decision. This landmark decision provided the most-often-cited legal definition of sexual harassment until the early 1990s.

More recent cases have broadened the definition of sexual harassment even further. In January 1991, an appellate court in Florida declared that nude pinups in the workplace could create a "hostile work environment" and thus be considered illegal. In this case, *Robinson* v. *Jacksonville Shipyards*, the court also concluded that the employer was directly liable for the sexual harassment. The judge in the case commented, "A pre-existing atmosphere that deters women from entering or continuing in a profession or job is no less destructive to and offensive to workplace equality than a sign declaring 'men only.'"

A week later, the Ninth Circuit Court of Appeals in San Francisco ruled that the courts should evaluate sexual harassment claims in light of a "reasonable woman" standard instead of the "reasonable person" standard ordinarily used. Traditionally, courts have accepted interpretations of events that conform to what a reasonable person would accept. The San Francisco court ruled that in the case of sexual harassment, a reasonable *woman* standard would be more appropriate because behavior that a man would find reasonable, a woman may define as sexual harassment. Webb notes, "This means that the victim's feelings must play a crucial role in identifying a series of actions as sexual harassment and that many employers will have to adopt a broader perspective in addressing sexual harassment complaints." The court also noted that the reasonable woman standard can be expected to change over time as the views of reasonable women change.

In November 1993, the Supreme Court heard its second case on sexual harassment, and again broadened the definition. In this case, *Harris* v. *Forklift Systems, Inc.*, the Supreme Court stated that to be found illegal a hostile work environment need not be psychologically harmful but only reasonably perceived as abusive. Thus, the current definition of sexual harassment is very different from that of the 1970s. No longer is sexual harassment considered the personal problem of the victim. It can now be an act of illegal discrimination when it is used in quid pro quo or hostile environment situations—and the definitions of such unacceptable situations have been radically expanded.

Many legal scholars and women's organizations consider the current legal definition of sexual harassment to be the appropriate response to a long-ignored problem. According to Diane Halpern, a California State University psychologist who specializes in gender differences, sexual harassment "destroys lives." Yet many businesspeople and ordinary citizens wonder if the definition of sexual harassment exaggerates the seriousness of the matter. One male plant manager contends, "The entire issue is a perfect example of a minor special interest group's ability to blow up an 'issue' to a level of importance which in no way relates to the reality of the world in which we live and work." And Daniel Seligman of *Fortune* magazine, commenting on the *Harris* decision, notes, "The parade of rulings has created a large anomaly in the law of the workplace. It has created a class of workers protected as no others are."

Since most of the complaints of sexual harassment are levied by women against men, in recent years "boys will be boys" has more often become "boys will be punished." But society's standards and the rules of the law and the courts are still far from congruence. At one end of the spectrum stand those who believe that the response to harassment is an absurd overreaction and that an adult should simply cope with or leave a situation where harassment is a problem. At another extreme stand those who would cite a construction worker for a wolf whistle or a suggestive remark, believing that everyone should be free from unwanted sexualized behavior. Scattered among them are many degrees of opinion, a wide range of which are represented in *At Issue: What Is Sexual Harassment?* The authors of the viewpoints in this volume continue the ongoing debate on how sexual harassment should be defined.

1

Sexual Harassment Should Be Defined Broadly

Susan L. Webb

Susan L. Webb is president of Pacific Resource Development Group, Inc., a Seattle-based consulting firm specializing in human relations issues. She is also the editor of the Webb Report, *a national newsletter on sexual harassment, and is the author of* Step Forward: Sexual Harassment in the Workplace.

Many people hear stories about sexual harassment and dismiss them as harmless or even amusing. But to those who experience it, sexual harassment can be very traumatic. For this reason, sexual harassment should be defined to include a wide range of behavior based on a behavioral definition and on a legal definition set forth by the Equal Employment Opportunity Commission (EEOC) and the courts.

A few years ago, a pertinent story appeared in the "Slice of Life" column of my local newspaper. ("Slice of Life" is where amusing, silly, or funny little stories are reported for everyone's daily amusement.) In this story, the woman, who worked for a rapid transit authority as a token clerk, claimed that she was subjected to continuous and repeated sexual comments by the general public because of an advertising poster that was behind her work station.

The poster advertised a health club with the caption "Have we got two great figures for you!" The first great figure was the $19.95 they charged to join the club, and the second was "Miss Pin-Up of 1983," lying on her side in a very small string bikini.

When I read the story, I, like most people, thought it was amusing and a little trivial, and I couldn't help thinking that some people—like this woman—really push the limits, that we were getting to the point where everything in the world is considered sexual harassment.

A few months later I heard another interesting story, this one about a pizza parlor whose employees had to wear animal costumes for the entertainment of their young customers. One table cleaner, who dressed like a squirrel, found some holes in her squirrel costume in what she thought were rather embarrassing places, so she took the outfit to her supervisor

Susan L. Webb, "Defining and Understanding Sexual Harassment," chapter 2 of *Step Forward: Sexual Harassment in the Workplace.* Published by MasterMedia, 1991. Copyright ©1991 Susan L. Webb. Reprinted with permission.

to get it repaired. Instead of having the uniform fixed, he began teasing her about boy squirrels and girl squirrels, saying he thought that the holes were in "squirrel-appropriate locations." The final straw for the employee was when her supervisor came up behind her and pantomimed what a boy squirrel would do to a girl squirrel if she had a hole in that particular spot. The person who told me this story was the squirrel's attorney, at a party.

Again, I had those same doubting thoughts: the things people do to each other at work are a constant source of amazement, but an attorney! Had we gone too far again? Do we really need an attorney involved in a case like this?

A third story was about a young woman who went into her boss's office one afternoon to pick up an adding machine. Her boss was sitting at his desk, talking with a male employee who was standing across the desk from him. The woman walked around behind her boss's desk and bent over to pick up the machine. Her boss turned around in his swivel chair, to find her rump right in front of his face. The personnel director of this company told me that, without thinking, on the spur of the moment, with no malicious intent whatsoever, the boss "bit the woman on the butt."

Stopping to think

If you're like most people, by now you're either shaking your head at these stories or smiling or laughing outright. But when people stop to think about harassment instead of just reacting, or when it happens to someone they're close to, like their wife or daughter, husband or son, then the situation changes.

Let's go back through those three stories, starting with the token clerk. If we assume that only twenty thousand people went through her work station on a daily basis and that only one of every hundred made some kind of sexual comment, that's two hundred comments in an eight-hour shift. Even if we assume that only one out of every two hundred made a comment, we're still talking about a hundred comments every single day. You can imagine how tired of that poster the woman was by noon of the first day, or how tired of it her husband was on the second evening, when he'd heard about nothing else for two days. The story's not quite so funny the second time around.

If sexual harassment occurred right in front of us, many of the women would call it harassment and many of the men would call it a joke.

As for the table cleaner in the pizza parlor, it turns out that it wasn't she who had hired the attorney, but her mommy and daddy. The little squirrel was only fifteen years old, and her parents didn't think it was one bit funny when her twenty-two-year-old supervisor pantomimed boy squirrels and girl squirrels behind the counter at ten o'clock at night, when it was just the two of them alone in the store. Not so funny when you think it might be your daughter, granddaughter, or niece.

And the woman who was bitten didn't complain to anyone because she didn't want to get her boss in trouble; in fact, they were friends. But three weeks later she went to the human resources office and quit. When the personnel director tried to find out why she was leaving, she started crying and told him the story. It seems that the man who witnessed the biting went out and told everyone in the warehouse what he'd seen and how funny it was. Since then, people the woman didn't know had been coming up to her and teasing her about teeth marks or bruises on her behind; people would laugh and giggle when she walked into the lunchroom; some had even asked to see the "tattoo on [her] ass." So she wasn't going to cause problems for anyone. She was embarrassed and very uncomfortable, and she'd decided just to leave. This funny, stupid story just doesn't seem so funny after all, does it?

Recognizing harassment

One early survey, published in 1981 in the *Harvard Business Review*, said that the real problem was not in defining sexual harassment but in recognizing it when it occurs. The results showed that men and women see sexual harassment very differently. Of course, now, with hindsight, that doesn't seem very surprising, but what it means is that if sexual harassment occurred right in front of us, many of the women would call it harassment and many of the men would call it a joke. And it's not even that simple, because opinions about what is and isn't harassment vary not just between men and women, but between men and men, and women and women.

Most often, people think of sexual harassment in two extremes. Many think that the only time it's sexual harassment is when a supervisor or manager says, "Sleep with me or you're fired." Of course that is sexual harassment—the most serious kind—but that is only the tip of the iceberg. At the other extreme are people who think or say that everything in the world is sexual harassment, and if you say "Hi, hon, how's it going?" that's sexual harassment and a suit could be filed against you. That's a slight exaggeration too.

We can think of sexual harassment in two different ways. First, there's what we call the behavioral definition: a common-sense, everyday way of looking at the problem. Second is what we'll call the legal definition: what the EEOC [Equal Employment Opportunity Commission] Guidelines and the courts define as illegal discrimination.

The behavioral or common-sense definition

The most common behavioral definition of sexual harassment is "deliberate and/or repeated sexual or sex-based behavior that is not welcome, not asked for, and not returned." There are three major elements and two qualifiers in this definition.

First of all, for it to be sexual harassment, *the behavior in question has to be sexual in nature or sex-based*. In other words, it's behavior with some sort of sexual connotation to it or behavior that occurs because of the victim's being male or female.

The range of behavior with sexual connotations is very wide, and the behavior doesn't necessarily mean that the perpetrator has the intent of having sex. We must think in terms of a continuum of sexual behavior, ranging from the least severe end—including joking, innuendoes, flirting, asking someone for a date—to the most serious end—forced fondling, attempted or actual rape, sexual assault.

As for sex-based behavior—occurring on account of sex or gender—it too can be light or severe. It is negative behavior that is directed at, or has an impact on, only one gender. Negative gender-related behavior can include men putting down the women or women making negative remarks about the men—in other words, a serious battle of the sexes at the job site.

One example I heard was the men saying to the women, "I can't believe your husband lets you work here," "This is man's work," "You should be home having babies," "You're here only because of the affirmative action program." These comments were not sexy or sexual, but were made because of gender or sex—the men didn't say this kind of thing to other men. When you see such a battle between the men and women, the more traditional type of sexual harassment is usually occurring too, or is not far behind. In terms of our first definition, you should consider this kind of behavior sexual harassment.

Second, *the behavior has to be deliberate and/or repeated.* Some forms of sexual behavior are so graphic and offensive that the first time they occur they are considered deliberate, inappropriate, and sometimes even illegal actions. There are other forms of behavior that must be repeated over and over again before they become harassment. Both are serious and damaging, but we tend to disagree over their being labeled "sexual harassment."

For it to be sexual harassment, the behavior in question has to be sexual in nature or sex-based.

Most of us would agree that such severe sexual behavior as forced fondling, attempted rape, and serious sexual slurs definitely is not permissible. Where we have the difficulty and disagreement is at the other end of the continuum. What one person takes as joking another finds offensive and degrading.

Keep in mind that even comments made in a joking manner may not be bothersome the first few times, but day after day, joke after joke, they cease to be funny or amusing to the person who's receiving them. While the behavior may not be considered illegal sexual harassment, it still has a negative and damaging impact on the employee subjected to it.

One way of looking at it is to remember that *the more severe the behavior is, the fewer times it needs to be repeated before reasonable people define it as harassment; the less severe it is, the more times it needs to be repeated.* This is one of the two qualifiers of the definition. The severity of the behavior must be considered in conjunction with the number of repetitions.

The third part of the definition is that *sexual harassment is not welcome, not asked for, and not returned.* We are not talking about mutual behavior that people engage in together or enjoy. What two people do that is mutual is simply that, mutual, and is usually permissible so long as it doesn't interfere with their work or create a hostile or offensive work environment for others. (I say *usually* because some mutual behavior that may not be defined as harassment—because it *is* mutual—nevertheless still is not permissible in the work environment: mutual buttocks grabbing, mutual graphic sexual jokes, etc.)

When considering the welcomeness of the behavior, some people try to place the sole responsibility for setting limits on the victim: "It's not sexual harassment unless she or he says so." That's not quite right.

If we go back to the sexual-behavior continuum, we can add the second qualifier: *the less severe the behavior is, the more responsibility the receiver has to speak up* (because some people like this kind of behavior); *the more severe it is, the less responsibility the receiver has to speak up* (the initiator of the behavior should be sensitive enough in the first place to know that it is inappropriate).

The three elements—sexual or sex-based, deliberate and/or repeated, and not welcome, asked for, or returned—along with the two qualifiers of varying degrees of repetition and varying responsibilities of the sender and receiver, make up a complete, and some say too broad, definition of sexual harassment. It is primarily those with a legal perspective who initially feel that this definition may cover too much.

This definition covers more than what a purely legal definition might. The point is that studies have shown that light harassment tends to get worse and become severe when it is not addressed and stopped. By including in your assessment a definition of harassment that includes light, moderate, and severe, you can resolve the situation now and, it is to be hoped, in the future as well.

As for particular types of sexual harassment, it may be verbal, nonverbal, or physical. Verbal jokes, cracks, comments, and remarks are probably the most common form of harassment—what you're likely to see most often in complaints and investigations. Nonverbal harassment can be just as serious: certain kinds of looks, gestures, leering, ogling, photographs or cartoons. Physical harassment such as touching, pinching, rubbing, or "accidentally" brushing against someone's breasts or buttocks can be the most severe form of harassment and can involve criminal charges.

It's also important to remember that sexual harassment is really about power. The harasser either thinks or knows, consciously or unconsciously, that he or she has more power than the harassee. If not, there would be no harassment—the harassee could turn to the harasser and demand that it stop and there would be no issue.

When asked why they file lawsuits or formal complaints outside their organizations—why they did not solve the problem in-house—victims of harassment give two reasons:

- "I didn't think anyone would take me seriously." This says that they felt powerless. They thought or knew that others would laugh or tell them they were being too sensitive.
- "I couldn't get it stopped any other way." This indicates that they were powerless to stop unwanted behavior.

Deciding whether sexual harassment has occurred

To determine whether behavior should be labeled sexual harassment, first compare it with the behavioral definition: deliberate and/or repeated sexual or sex-based behavior that is not welcome, not asked for, and not returned. Do this analysis for each incident or act, then consider the overall picture.

1. Was the behavior sexual (about sex) or sex-based (on account of sex or directed to or affecting only one sex or gender)? First, plot each occurrence on the continuum so you have some picture of its severity:

> • Potentially harassing behavior has the potential to be sexual harassment, particularly if repeated enough times, but it can also be socially acceptable in certain situations. This behavior is more likely to be called inappropriate or out of line, but not truly ha-

rassment, especially if just one instance has occurred.

- Subtle sexual behavior is sometimes socially acceptable, but some reasonable men and women would see it as offensive and want it stopped. The receivers usually don't want anything done to the sender at this point, other than making him or her stop. The behavior is bothersome, worth mentioning, but would not warrant a formal complaint if it were all that occurred.

- Moderate sexual behavior is not socially acceptable, and reasonable men and women see it as offensive and would want it stopped. The behavior is serious enough that some action must be taken against the sender (such as warning letters or reprimands), in addition to having him or her stop the behavior. The behavior is offensive and could warrant a complaint even if it were all that occurred.

- Severe sexual behavior is never socially acceptable and is so graphic or severe that one instance can call for serious disciplinary action, such as probation, suspension, or termination of the offending employee(s). Included in this category is physical behavior such as attempted or actual rape or sexual assault and verbal behavior such as serious sexual slurs.

2. Was the behavior deliberate and/or repeated? If it was not deliberate—truly accidental—then you most likely cannot label it harassment at all. If it was not accidental, then how often was it repeated? Remember the qualifier: the less severe the behavior, the more repetitions required to label it harassment; the more severe, the fewer repetitions needed. Also keep in mind that repeated instances of similar behavior can constitute repetitions: three different sexual remarks could be the same as three repetitions of one comment.

What one person takes as joking another finds offensive and degrading.

3. Was the behavior welcome, asked for, or returned? Again, remember the qualifier: the less severe the behavior, the more the responsibility of the receiver to speak up; the more severe, the less responsibility the receiver has to speak up and the more responsibility the sender has to monitor his or her own behavior. Did the receiver tell or indicate to the sender that the behavior was unwelcome? Was it necessary that the receiver give notice, or should the sender have known better in the first place?

If the behavior was reciprocated in any way, was there a balance between the seriousness of the sender's behavior and the receiver's response? One of the arguments you will hear is that the complainant employee liked the behavior, engaged in it himself or herself, asked for it, encouraged it, etc. If this is the case, then both (or all) of the parties should be talked to so that this type of behavior is stopped (though it is not to be labeled sexual harassment, since it was welcome). However, first determine whether there was a balance between the sender's behavior and the receiver's response.

For example, if the alleged victim was telling off-color jokes in response to the alleged harasser's telling off-color jokes, then it would appear that the jokes were welcome and there was a balance in terms of severity of the conduct. But if the sender of the jokes used the receiver's telling of jokes as an invitation to go to a higher or more severe level—such as physical grabbing of buttocks or breasts—then the balance has shifted and the argument is not justified. Consider the balance in the severity of the behavior.

The definition according to the EEOC Guidelines and the courts

The second step in determining whether sexual harassment has occurred is to consider each behavior, then the overall picture, in light of the EEOC Guidelines. There are several key points of the Guidelines that need to be considered. These key points plus court decisions provide the legal definition of sexual harassment and spell out the rights and responsibilities of employers and employees. State laws may also pertain.

1. Section A of the Guidelines says that unwelcome sexual advances, requests for sexual favors, and other verbal or physical conduct of a sexual nature constitutes sexual harassment under any of four conditions:

- When such behavior is either explicitly or implicitly part of a manager's or supervisor's decision to hire or fire someone. When submitting to sexual conduct is a term or condition of employment, it is illegal, whether the request or demand was made outright or simply implied. Showing that such a request was implied might involve looking at employment records before and after the request was rejected. When an action amounts to the same thing as an explicit request, it too is illegal.

- When such behavior is used to make other employment decisions such as pay, promotion, or job assignment. Any time an employment decision is based on whether an employee submitted or refused to submit to some form of sexual conduct, it is illegal. The employment decision does not have to actually cost the employee his or her job, nor does the sexual conduct have to be an actual request for sex. The supervisor who plays favorites with workers who go along with his habit of telling dirty jokes or making sexual comments and bends the rules in their favor is making employment decisions based on willingness to submit to sexual conduct.

These two conditions are what courts have called quid pro quo harassment: someone with the power to do so, usually a supervisor or manager, offers some kind of tangible job benefit for submission to sexual harassment. In these cases courts have held the employer strictly liable—responsible even when the employer did not know the harassment was occurring and even if it had a policy forbidding such behavior.

- When such behavior has the purpose or effect of unreasonably interfering with the employee's work performance.

- When such behavior creates an intimidating, hostile, or offensive work environment.

Courts have called these two conditions hostile environment harassment: the damage caused by the sexual behavior does not have to be a tangible economic consequence such as losing the job or promotion, but the atmosphere at work becomes so negative that it affects the employee's ability to do his or her job. The sexual behavior is illegal harassment.

The EEOC included the words *purpose or effect* to indicate that intent to harm is not a necessary element of sexual harassment. If an employee's unwanted sexual behavior has the effect of creating a hostile work environment and interfering with another employee's work performance, the first employee's intent may be irrelevant.

To fit the EEOC's definition, sexual harassment must have two characteristics: it is unwelcome and unwanted and it has an impact on an employee's job or work environment. Whether the sexual behavior is directed to an employee face-to-face or behind his or her back, and whether the behavior occurs during breaks or in locker rooms, may not be important so long as it has an impact on the employee's work environment.

2. Section B says that each claim of sexual harassment should be examined on a case-by-case basis. Consideration should be given to the context in which the behavior took place, the nature of the sexual behavior, and the record as a whole.

Liability for harassment

3. Sections C and D have to do with the employer's liability. Section C says that the employer may be held "strictly liable" for harassment by supervisors—meaning even when the employer is not aware of the harassment and even when there is a policy forbidding such behavior. Section D says that the employer is liable for co-worker harassment when the employer knows of the harassment and fails to take immediate and appropriate action.

Several courts ruled in 1983 that "strict liability" applies only in quid pro quo harassment cases, in which a tangible job benefit was affected, and the victim can file a charge without notifying management of the harassment. If it is hostile environment harassment, the victim must allow the employer the opportunity to take appropriate action before the victim can file a complaint. This issue is still being addressed by the courts.

4. Section E says that the employer may be held responsible for sexual harassment of its employees by people who are nonemployees—such as customers or the general public—when the employer knows about the harassment and does nothing. In these cases the extent of the employer's control over the situation is examined closely, and if in any way the employer can stop the harassment, it is responsible for doing so.

5. Section F says that employers should take all necessary steps to prevent sexual harassment from occurring in the first place. This includes policy statements, training for employees, and grievance procedures.

Light harassment tends to get worse and become severe when it is not addressed and stopped.

---

6. Section G says that if one employee submits to sexual requests and gains benefits thereby, other employees, equally well qualified, may sue on the basis of sex discrimination for not being allowed those same benefits or opportunities. If a supervisor gives the best job assignments to a subordinate because of their sexual activities, other employees, both male and female, could claim sex discrimination because they were denied those job assignments. This section of the Guidelines was upheld by a federal court in Delaware.

But the question, what does the law say, is just like the other questions—it has no simple answer either. What "the law" says can be interpreted to mean what the EEOC Guidelines say, what the 1964 Civil Rights Act says, what the courts are saying, or a combination of all three. A good basic answer is to think in these terms—for behavior to be considered illegal sexual harassment, it must meet these criteria:

- It occurs because of the person's sex—it is related to or about sex.

- It is unwelcome, not returned, not mutual.

- It affects the terms or conditions of employment, including the work environment itself.

Summary

The most widely used, common-sense definition of sexual harassment is "deliberate and/or repeated sexual or sex-based behavior that is not welcome, not asked for, and not returned."

The less severe behavior is, the more times it must be repeated before it is considered sexual harassment.

The more severe behavior is, the fewer times it must be repeated before it is considered sexual harassment.

The less severe behavior is, the more responsibility the receiver has to speak up and make it known that it is offensive or unwelcome.

The more severe behavior is, the less responsibility the receiver has to speak up, and the more responsibility the perpetrator of the behavior has to know better than to engage in that behavior in the first place.

The EEOC Guidelines state that unwanted sexual advances, requests for sexual favors, and other verbal or physical actions of a sexual nature become illegal when connected to a manager's or supervisor's decision regarding hiring, firing, pay, promotion, job assignment, or other aspect of employment, or when such sexual behavior interferes with an employee's ability to perform work or creates a hostile, offensive work environment.

2

The Definition of Sexual Harassment Applies to Schools

Nan Stein

Nan Stein worked for the Massachusetts Department of Education for 14 years on sex equity and civil rights matters. She now works for the Center for Research on Women at Wellesley College in Wellesley, Massachusetts. She is the author of Gender and Education, *published by the National Society for the Study of Education.*

Definitions of sexual harassment are usually applied to the workplace. Sexual harassment also occurs in elementary and secondary schools, however, where it inhibits education and can be just as damaging as that which occurs in the workplace. Teachers and administrators must be trained to recognize sexual harassment and take steps to prevent it.

The only Latin teacher in the high school often touches his students. The entire class once saw him lie on top of a female student on her desk and rub his private organs against her upper arm. The student became upset, began to cry, and left the room in search of the principal.

The teacher later apparently admitted his guilt to the principal, but received no formal punishment. None of the students who witnessed the incident was questioned or interviewed by school authorities or anyone else. Nor were they informed of the consequences for the teacher.

That teacher still teaches the class, and the students who witnessed the incident remain his students. The girl who was involved stayed in the class for a while, but her lingering feelings eventually caused her to drop out. She was not able to finish the course with another teacher since the school had no other Latin teachers.—*Testimony by a 12th-grade male high school student in Montana, November 1991*

"I started being sexually harassed constantly by a group of guys on my bus. It was horrible. It lasted the whole year and some of eighth grade without anything being done about it. They would grab my breasts, thighs, and other places, and make rude comments and sexual gestures toward me.

Nan Stein, "What Is Sexual Harassment?" *The School Administrator*, January 1993. Copyright ©1993 American Association of School Administrators. Reprinted with permission.

"When I finally yelled at them to stop, hit them, or moved away, the bus driver would yell at me. I felt helpless because my parents worked and couldn't drive me to school. Finally, I got the courage to do something about it: I told my principal what was happening. He was skeptical about the whole thing, and he didn't do much about it."—*Report of a 14-year-old girl from Pennsylvania*

A 25-year-old coach and social studies teacher is romantically involved with a 16-year-old student in his world cultures class. Although he appears to treat her impartially in class interactions, there's a rumor that since their involvement, she has been getting straight A's, compared to the B's and C's she received before.

The scuttlebutt in the teachers' lounge suggests the teacher's behavior is inappropriate, yet the young woman's parents are flattered such a nice, successful young man has taken up with their daughter.—*Consolidated from news accounts*

Sexual harassment is a form of sex discrimination, and is illegal as defined by Title IX of the Educational Amendments of 1972.

A group of seventh- and eighth-grade girls repeatedly were molested by a male teacher in the school cafeteria during lunch period. He squats down at their lunch table and walks his fingers up the inside of their thighs, saying all the while, "Are you chicken?" He also tickles them, massages their shoulders, and touches the sides of their breasts.

Other adults were present, but everyone liked to describe his behavior as "horseplay" or "teasing." When one girl reported his behavior to her female guidance counselor, she was told, "He wouldn't do that. He's such a friendly religious man."

Not one adult, all of whom were "mandated reporters," ever reported "Lester the Molester" to the state agency responsible for investigating allegations of child sexual abuse.—*Depositions from J.O. v. the Alton, Ill., Community Unit School District*

These accounts of sexual harassment and child sexual abuse in schools are not atypical. They are repeated daily across the country in every kind of community, from large urban centers to small rural communities and privileged suburban towns.

These stories are located in the folklore and oral histories of schools that are passed along by students or school personnel. They also come from testimonials from teachers, parents, and students who witness or experience sexual harassment. They can be found in the public record, gleaned from court documents and newspaper accounts of pending lawsuits or complaints.

Public awakening

As a workplace issue, sexual harassment has received wider exposure nationally since the televised Senate hearings involving Clarence Thomas and Anita Hill in fall 1991. That public awakening preceded the U.S. Supreme Court's 9-0 decision in February 1992 in *Franklin v. Gwinnett County (Ga.) Public Schools.* This case informed the nation's educational institutions for the first time that they are liable for compensatory damages under Title IX, the 20-year-old federal law that guarantees an educational environment free from sex discrimination.

Sexual harassment is a form of sex discrimination, and is illegal as defined by Title IX of the Educational Amendments of 1972, Title VII of the Civil Rights Act, the 14th Amendment of the Constitution, and numerous state criminal and civil statutes.

Students and employees are legally protected against sexual harassment.

Students and employees are legally protected against sexual harassment, regardless of whether the perpetrator is an employee, a student, or an individual connected to the school district only by being part of an organization with which the school has a contractual agreement.

Some forms of sexual harassment also may be actionable as child abuse, sexual assault, rape, pornography, criminal or civil libel, slander, or defamation of character. Victims, as well as educators or community members acting on the victim's behalf, may file sexual harassment complaints.

Peer-to-peer sexual harassment is rampant in elementary and secondary schools. Examples include students' attempts to pull down gym shorts or flip up skirts; the circulation of "summa cum slutty" or "piece of the ass of the week" lists; designation of "national sexual harassment week"; nasty, personalized graffiti on bathroom walls; sexualized jokes that mock women's bodies; bras snapped and body parts groped; and outright physical assault and attempted rape.

Sometimes identified and curtailed, these behaviors more often than not are allowed to continue recklessly and deliberately. Sexual harassment is tolerated as a true-blooded, healthy American phenomenon, a normal stage in adolescent development. Often it is labeled as "flirting" or as "initiation rites" that must be tolerated. "No harm done," rings the claim. Regardless of how its appearances and existence are rationalized, sexual harassment interferes with the right to receive an equal educational opportunity.

Criminal behavior

When the specter or hint of a sexually tinged relationship between a minor and an adult in a school setting emerges, confusion or cover-up is the typical response. Because the sexual harassment has entered a new domain, that of child abuse and criminal felonious behavior, more legally is at stake.

Despite the lack of extensive documented occurrences in public schools, incidents of sexual abuse and sexual harassment happen, and the offenders frequently are clustered in a few particular capacities within the school community.

Roles such as coach, physical education teacher, music teacher, driver education teacher, and extracurricular club adviser often require individual contact with students, often in private settings, and often in a capacity that builds trust and intimacy between an adult and students.

Although these same adults may serve in a dual capacity as classroom teachers, evidence suggests physical sexual harassment from these individuals occurs less frequently when they are in their public classroom roles as opposed to when they are operating in their adjunctive, more private roles.

In cases of alleged child sexual abuse of a minor by a school employee, school officials often bypass the legal requirement to report these allegations to the state agency charged with investigating such allegations. School officials sometimes decide they will conduct the first round of investigation for reasons of expediency and proximity. More likely, their failure or delay to report the allegations may be driven by their desire not to hang their dirty laundry in public or to protect the accused, one of their own.

None of these motives, however, exempts educators from the legal requirement to report allegations of inappropriate physical contact between an adult and a student to the proper state authorities, who are empowered to pursue the investigation.

Reports are dismissed

Unfortunately, reports to those state agencies charged with protecting children from child abuse and neglect frequently are dismissed after a required period of investigation. Agencies responsible for child welfare and protection, saddled with constant staff shortages and high case loads, are limited in their authority to remove children from abusive and neglectful homes. Thus, insult is added to injury when there is an attempt to report the alleged occurrence of child sexual abuse in a school setting. Jurisdictional confusion, gaps in policy, and a virtual "no man's land" exist, thus vitiating many allegations of child sexual abuse in schools.

Meanwhile, problems in schools fester, spawning an atmosphere that permits and tolerates, at a minimum, sexual harassment and discrimination, denying students the right to an equal educational opportunity and equal protection under the law.

Other more cynical lessons also are taught by such behaviors: schools become unsafe places and students lose confidence in school policies and trust for school officials. These consequences are felt not only by victims and subjects, but also by bystanders, whether they are innocent witnesses or deliberate colluders.

Occasionally, sexual harassment is reported to those rare school officials who do indeed believe that such allegations warrant pursuit, but often find themselves "ad-libbing," inventing a system of investigation and adjudication. At other times, these same school officials, frustrated by their institution's inability or unwillingness to pursue these allegations, may turn to state agencies charged with resolving complaints of sex discrimination (agencies such as the state education department or the state's human rights commission). At the very least, an intervention from an outside agency may escalate the situation, and often leads to more litigious remedies than those that might have been applied successfully had they occurred at the school level at an earlier stage of the conflict.

Mobile molesters

A mobile molester is created when the superintendent or school board works out a backroom deal with a teacher or administrator who has been accused of molestation or improper sexual conduct with a minor.

The arrangement typically includes a voluntary letter of resignation from the accused in return for a letter of reference from the school system. No dismissal proceedings are held, the state education department is not informed, and the accused's teaching certificate remains intact.

Armed with a letter of reference, the mobile molester moves along to another unsuspecting community where the accused is likely to repeat the alleged behaviors again. More than one culprit emerges from such scenarios because the mobile molester is a creation of a duplicitous superintendent and school board who prefer to pass along a harasser rather than proceed with dismissal proceedings.

In such cases, the superintendent and the school board are guilty at the very least of having created a negligent reference, and more likely, of putting more children in harm's way. Such conspiracies of silence and commission must stop, even if it takes prosecution for negligence.

Simple remedies

The cases cited at the beginning of this viewpoint are simultaneously mundane and extreme. They also indicate the negligence of school authorities who should have known and should have intervened. To rectify such neglect and to educate the entire school community, mandated professional development workshops and seminars are needed. Everyone in the school community, including the custodian, bus driver, classroom teacher, coach, extracurricular adviser, superintendent, and school board member must be trained to recognize sexual harassment, to know about his or her responsibilities to report it to the proper individuals and agencies, and to create strategies to prevent and eliminate it.

Along with other sustained, multipronged educational efforts, school leaders can crack the denial or casualness that surrounds sexual harassment in schools. Ongoing professional development for those who work or plan to work in any capacity in the schools must be offered and required to prevent and eliminate sexual harassment.

In addition, policies and grievance mechanisms must be written in language that is accessible to all students. Students should be included in the ongoing conversations about sexual harassment and child sexual abuse in schools through orientation assemblies and handbooks, support/rap groups, peer advising, and activities infused into the curriculum. Both male and female adults should be trained and designated to serve as "ombuds," available to the students.

Sexual harassment, a well-known social secret, must become a public concern if it is to be obliterated from educational settings. Only then will our schools be safe and conducive learning environments for all students, with equal educational opportunities and justice available for females and males.

To live out democracy, we need to practice it in our schools.

Notes

Cohan, Audrey (1991). *Child sexual abuse within the schools*. Unpublished doctoral dissertation, Hofstra University, Hempstead, N.Y.

Franklin v. Gwinnett County School District, ___U.S. ___, 112 S. Ct. 1028 (1992).

Linn, Eleanor, Stein, Nan, & Young, Jackie, with Sandra Davis (1992). "Bitter lessons for all: sexual harassment in schools." In James T. Sears (Ed.), *Sex-

uality and the Curriculum (pp. 149–174). New York: Teacher's College Press.

Massachusetts Department of Education, Bureau of Educational Resources and Television (1982). *No laughing matter: High school students and sexual harassment.* 1385 Hancock Street, Quincy, MA 02169-5183.

Minnesota Department of Education (1988). *It's not fun/it's illegal. The identification and prevention of sexual harassment to teenagers. A curriculum.* 522 Capitol Square Building, 55 Cedar Street, St. Paul, MN 55101.

Northwest Women's Law Center (1992). *Sexual harassment in Employment and Education* (a manual). Northwest Women's Law Center, 119 S. Main Street, Suite 330, Seattle, WA 98104-2515.

Regotti, Terri L. (1992). Negligent hiring and retaining of sexually abusive teachers. *Education Law Reporter*, May 21, 333–340.

Sorenson, Gail Paulus (1991). "Sexual Abuse in Schools: Reported court cases from 1987–1990." *Educational Administration Quarterly*, 27(4), 460-480.

Stein, Nan, "Sexual Harassment in Elementary and Secondary Education." Biklen and Pollard (Eds.), *Gender and Education.* 1993. National Society for the Study of Education, Yearbook 1993.

Stein, Nan (Ed.). (1986—4th edition) *Who's Hurt and Who's Liable: Sexual Harassment in Massachusetts Schools.* Quincy: Massachusetts Department of Education, Civil Rights/Chapter 622 Project, 1385 Hancock Street, Quincy, MA 02169-5183. (original work published in 1979).

University of Michigan, Programs for Educational Opportunity (1985). *Tune in Your Rights: A guide for teenagers about turning off sexual harassment.* 1005 School of Education, University of Michigan, Ann Arbor, MI 48109-1259.

Wishnietsky, Dan (1991). "Reported and unreported teacher-student sexual harassment." *Journal of Educational Research*, January/February, 84:3, 164-169.

3

The "Reasonable Woman" Definition of Sexual Harassment Makes Sense

Ellen Goodman

Ellen Goodman is a nationally syndicated columnist with the Boston Globe.

While many ordinary people are unclear about how to define sexual harassment, the courts have established a legal definition. They increasingly are applying a "reasonable woman" test to determine if sexual harassment has occurred. According to the "reasonable woman" standard, if a reasonable woman defines a given situation as sexual harassment, then it is sexual harassment. Men and women, not just the courts, can understand what constitutes sexual harassment by looking at it from the point of view of a "reasonable woman."

Since the volatile mix of sex and harassment exploded under the Capitol dome, it hasn't just been senators scurrying for cover. The case of the professor and judge [Anita Hill and Clarence Thomas] has left a gender gap that looks more like a crater.

Men and women see differently

We have discovered that men and women see this issue differently. Stop the presses. Sweetheart, get me rewrite.

On the *Today* show, Bryant Gumbel asks something about a man's right to have a pinup on the wall and Katie Couric says what she thinks of that. On the normally sober *MacNeil/Lehrer* hour the usual panel of legal experts doesn't break down between left and right but between male and female.

On a hundred radio talk shows, women are sharing experiences and men are asking for proof. In ten thousand offices, the order of the day is the nervous joke. One boss asks his secretary if he can still say "good morning," or is that sexual harassment. Heh, heh. The women aren't laughing.

Okay boys and girls, back to your corners. Can we talk? Can we hear?

Ellen Goodman, "The Reasonable Woman Standard," *Liberal Opinion Weekly*, October 21, 1991. Copyright ©1991, The Boston Globe Newspaper Co./Washington Post Writers Group. Reprinted with permission.

The good news is that women have stopped rolling their eyes at each other and started speaking out. The bad news is that we may each assume the other gender not only doesn't understand but can't understand. "They don't get it" becomes "they can't get it."

Let's start with the fact that sexual harassment is a concept as new as date rape. Date rape, that should-be oxymoron, assumes a different perspective on the part of the man and the woman. His date, her rape. Sexual harassment comes with some of the same assumptions. What he labels sexual, she labels harassment.

This produces what many men tend to darkly call a "murky" area of the law. Murky however is a step in the right direction. When everything was clear, it was clearly biased. The old single standard was male standard. The only options a working woman had were to grin, bear it or quit.

Emerging rules

Sexual harassment rules are based on the point of view of the victim, nearly always a woman. The rules ask, not just whether she has been physically assaulted, but whether the environment in which she works is intimidating or coercive. Whether she feels harassed. It says that her feelings matter.

This of course raises all sorts of hackles about women's *feelings*, women's *sensitivity*. How can you judge the sensitivity level of every single woman you work with? What's a poor man to do?

But the law isn't psychiatry. It doesn't adapt to individual sensitivity levels. There is a standard emerging by which the courts can judge these cases and by which people can judge them as well. It's called "the reasonable woman standard." How would a reasonable woman interpret this? How would a reasonable woman behave?

This is not an entirely new idea, although perhaps the law's belief in the reasonableness of women is. There has long been a "reasonable man" in the law, not to mention a "reasonable pilot," a "reasonable innkeeper," a "reasonable train operator."

Now the law is admitting that a reasonable woman may see these situations differently than a man. That truth—available in your senator's mailbag—is also apparent in research. We tend to see sexualized situations from our own gender's perspective. Kim Lane Scheppele, a political science and law professor at the University of Michigan, summarizes the miscues this way: "Men see the sex first and miss the coercion. Women see the coercion and miss the sex."

> *We tend to see sexualized situations from our own gender's perspective.*

Does that mean that we are genetically doomed to our double vision? Scheppele is quick to say no. Our justice system rests on the belief that one person can get in another's head, walk in her shoes, see things from another perspective. And so does our hope for change.

If a jury of car drivers can understand how a "reasonable pilot" would see one situation, a jury of men can see how a reasonable woman would see another event. The crucial ingredient is empathy.

Check it out in the office tomorrow. He's coming on, she's backing off, he keeps coming. Read the body language. There's a playboy calendar on the wall and a PMS joke in the boardroom and the boss is just being friendly. How would a reasonable woman feel?

At this moment, when the air is crackling with hostility and consciousness-raising has the hair sticking up on the back of many necks, guess what? Men can "get it." Reasonable men.

Businesses Should Clearly Define Sexual Harassment

Kara Swisher

Kara Swisher is a staff writer for the Washington Post.

The 1991 Clarence Thomas–Anita Hill hearings prompted a national discussion of sexual harassment. In the wake of the hearings, the number of sexual harassment complaints increased and, seeing the potential for expensive lawsuits, many corporations implemented policies explicitly proscribing sexual harassment. Whether businesses have existing anti-harassment policies or are just designing them, they should clearly define sexual harassment and outline procedures to follow if it occurs.

A revolution in the American workplace began in 1986, when the Supreme Court ruled that sexual harassment is a form of job discrimination. Five years later came Anita Hill's stunning accusations against Clarence Thomas, which acted as a lightning rod for the anger millions of women had felt about the problem, but had rarely dared to express.

The issue is by now so burned into the nation's consciousness that this season's [1993–94] runaway bestseller is Michael Crichton's *Disclosure*, which features a man-bites-dog turnabout in which the sexual harasser is a woman, nicknamed "Meredith Manmuncher." The book is now jokingly being called *Harassic Park*, after Crichton's bestseller about dinosaurs.

But the next step in this revolution—and one that is likely to be far more powerful than any book or congressional hearing—is how ever-clearer definitions of sexual harassment are being implemented by more and more corporations around the country. As this happens, an increasing number of companies are searching for better ways to protect themselves, laying down their own laws to stop behavior that isn't just unwanted, but is also illegal.

"We are pretty much telling our clients that they could be held legally responsible anymore if they don't try to go out and do something," says Douglas McDowell, general counsel for the Equal Employment Advisory Council, which represents nearly 300 Fortune 500 companies nationwide. "The worst thing anymore to do is nothing."

Kara Swisher, "Corporations Are Seeing the Light on Harassment," *The Washington Post National Weekly Edition*, February 14-20, 1994. Copyright ©1994, The Washington Post. Reprinted with permission.

Adds Diane Generous, director of risk management for the National Association of Manufacturers: "Any smart employer is going to listen."

Harassment costs

Statistics explain why companies are taking the issue so seriously. Most surveys indicate that sexual harassment claims have roughly doubled since 1991. Complaints filed with the Equal Employment Opportunity Commission [EEOC] have grown from 3,300 in 1991 to about 7,300 in 1993.

The vast majority of these claims involve men as harassers. And most of the women complainants say that they were victimized by a "hostile" work environment in which lewd sexual comments were tolerated, rather than by blatant "quid pro quo" demands for sex. According to the New York–based workplace research group Catalyst, recent studies have found that 40 percent to 60 percent of women say they have been sexually harassed sometime in their career.

As for the *Disclosure* plot twist about a menacing female manager, "It is just so rare a scenario," says Los Angeles attorney Gloria Allred.

She scoffs at Crichton's premise even though she made recent headlines winning an unprecedented $1 million for a California man who said he was harassed by a female supervisor. "Sure it happens, but it's probably more likely as fiction."

The penalties for sexual harassers—and companies that tolerate them—are about to get considerably tougher. A recent Supreme Court ruling makes it easier for victims to win cases. On the way are proposed new federal regulations that could define sexual harassment more clearly. And Congress is considering legislation that would lift the caps on damages that can be awarded in sexual harassment suits.

Ever-clearer definitions of sexual harassment are being implemented by more and more corporations around the country.

"Let's face it, sexual harassment does not add to the bottom line, and a really sophisticated company now has a lot of guidelines that are easy to comply with," says Steve Bokat, general counsel for the U.S. Chamber of Commerce and executive vice president of the National Chamber Litigation Center, the business group's public policy arm. So what should a wise CEO do to stop sexual harassment in the workplace? Experts offer a range of advice:

- The most important element, the experts say, is a senior management that makes clear to workers that harassment in any form won't be tolerated. If top managers don't take the issue seriously, workplace consultants explain, employees won't either. Managers must also understand that they are accountable for actions of their subordinates.
- Companies need an explicit written policy on sexual harassment that is widely disseminated in the workplace. Most consultants advise companies to do more than just post the policy on bulletin boards. They should distribute it companywide, repeatedly. Copies should be included in new employee orientation packets.

- Employees should have clear definitions of what sexual harassment is—and isn't. Consultants say that in this transitional time, employees may think harassment is occurring where it is not. A stray rude joke or pat on the shoulder is typically not harassment, say experts, though a confused work environment may make it seem so.
  Glassmaker Corning Inc. and many others, for example, have made videotapes depicting different harassing scenes. At the First Boston investment firm, employees now must sign a compliance statement that pledges they have received, read and intend to comply with the company's sexual harassment policies.
- Many companies are now offering employee training sessions. Chemical giant DuPont Co. is famous for its 24-hour sexual harassment hotline and its four-hour "A Matter of Respect" program that most of its employees have attended and that is being marketed to other companies. Follow-up training also is a good idea, many say.
- Training programs should include all employees, rather than just managers. The tone should be gender-neutral (including female harassers, as in the Crichton book) and avoid heavy-handed discussions of male harassment that may cause resentment among male workers. Often, many experts say, men who abhor sexual harassment end up feeling attacked in training programs—weakening the programs' effectiveness.
- Companies need a good system to deal with complaints. A clear process for handling complaints shows that a company takes them seriously; a sloppy or haphazard process can make the problem much worse.

The first rule, according to several consultants, is to move quickly when a complaint is received. Managers should not attempt to dissuade a complainant from making a report. Instead, they should arrange a careful investigation, in which credible co-workers are interviewed and the accused is given an opportunity to respond to the charges.

If the investigation reveals sexual harassment, a swift and clear disciplinary action should be taken—ranging from therapy to suspension to firing. If nothing is done to a harasser, employees know immediately that there are no teeth behind the bark. If an accused person is found innocent, experts advise being clear and forthright with employees about that too.

Every day, it becomes more unacceptable to sexually harass, because there are more punishments and sanctions.

The modern legal view of sexual harassment dates back to the Supreme Court's 1986 ruling in *Meritor Bank v. Vinson*, a case that will go down as the *Roe v. Wade* of workplace harassment. Affirming Title VII of the Civil Rights Act of 1964, the court ruled that employers must protect workers from discriminatory intimidation and ridicule—and specified that sexual harassment is a form of job discrimination that prevents a worker from enjoying equal employment opportunity.

The EEOC soon bolstered that ruling by requiring the companies take "immediate and appropriate corrective action" in cases of harassment.

Congress added more teeth in the 1991 Civil Rights Act by allowing victims to collect monetary damages—capped at $300,000—from employers for such things as distress, illness, medical costs and loss of employment caused by harassment.

Even with all this law, it took the media glare of the 1991 Anita Hill–Clarence Thomas hearings to bring the issue of sexual harassment into clear focus for most Americans.

"It was a sea change, even though the law has been evolving," says Marcia Greenberger, co-president of the National Women's Law Center. "It was a landmark in the societal and corporate understanding of sexual harassment and the laws in place to stop it."

The next legal milestone was the Supreme Court's unanimous ruling in November 1993 in *Harris v. Forklift Systems Inc.*, which made it much easier for victims of sexual harassment to make a legal case by disallowing the need to prove "severe psychological injury" caused by harassment.

Writing for the court, Justice Sandra Day O'Connor argued that protection under federal law "comes into play before the harassing conduct leads to a nervous breakdown."

Business groups, which typically shun more federal meddling, welcomed the decision.

"It didn't change the law that was really there already," says McDowell of the Equal Employment Advisory Council. "But business reaction was positive because it helps them by giving them another more clear piece of information."

Business could get more guidance soon, when the EEOC releases a new set of rules that is likely to define a "hostile work environment" as one where an employer fails to establish an "explicit policy against harassment."

Some of the proposed guidelines defining a hostile workplace reportedly would include certain types of rude remarks, negative stereotyping, threatening, intimidating or hostile acts, and written or graphic material that denigrates a protected group.

And Congress could up the ante for companies that harbor harassers if it passes the proposed Equal Remedies Act, which would remove the caps on monetary damages that can be awarded in federal cases of sexual harassment.

"I think that companies are starting to get the message," says Judith Lichtman, president of the Women's Legal Defense Fund. "Every day, it becomes more unacceptable to sexually harass, because there are more punishments and sanctions, damages to pay, jobs lost and it will all affect the bottom line."

5
Sexual Harassment Definitions Apply to Academia

Michele A. Paludi and Richard B. Barickman

Michele A. Paludi, a developmental psychologist, is director of women's studies at Hunter College of the City University of New York. Paludi has edited Ivory Power: Sexual Harassment on Campus *and co-edited* Academic and Workplace Sexual Harassment: A Resource Manual *with Richard B. Barickman, an associate professor of English at Hunter College.*

There are two types of definitions of sexual harassment. The first is the legal definition, spelled out by the Equal Employment Opportunity Commission (EEOC). It covers both quid pro quo harassment, where a superior demands sexual favors from an employee in exchange for continued employment or benefits, and hostile environment harassment, where one employee poisons the work atmosphere of another with sexual or gender-specific comments. The second definition of sexual harassment is empirical. It includes five levels of sexual harassment on a scale ranging from generalized statements and behavior to rape. These definitions apply both to the workplace and to academia.

What is sexual harassment?
Do you feel that the following experiences illustrate forms of sexual harassment?

> Dr. P. gave me the creeps. Whenever we took a test, I'd look up from my paper, and there he would be, staring at my top or my legs. I quit wearing skirts to that class because I was so uncomfortable around him. I felt like I was some kind of freak in a zoo.

> Dr. Y. asked me if I wished to share a motel room with him at meetings to be held in the spring. Following our return from these meetings (at which I did not share a motel room with him), he began criticizing my work, suggesting that there was something wrong with my master's thesis data, suggesting that my experimental groups would not replicate, etc. (Dziech & Weiner, 1984)

Reprinted from *Academic and Workplace Sexual Harassment: A Resource Manual* by Michele A. Paludi and Richard B. Barickman by permission of the State University of New York Press. Copyright ©1991 by State University of New York.

I was discussing my work in a public setting when a professor cut me off and asked if I had freckles all over my body.

He (the teaching assistant) kept saying, "Don't worry about the grade," and, "You know we'll settle everything out of class."

I see male colleagues and professors chum it up and hear all the talk about making the old boy network operate for women, so I thought nothing of accepting an invitation from a . . . professor to attend a gathering at his house. Other graduate students were present. . . . The professor made a fool out of himself pursuing me (it took me a while to catch on) and then blurted, "You know I want to sleep with you; I have a great deal of influence. Now, of course I don't want to force you into anything, but I'm sure you're going to be sensible about this." I fled.

Playboy centerfolds were used as Anatomy teaching slides. . . . In slides, lectures, teaching aids and even in our own student note service, we found that nurses were presented as sexy, bitchy, or bossy but never as professional health care workers.

The financial officer made it clear that I could get the money I needed if I slept with him. (U.S. Department of Education, Office for Civil Rights, pamphlet, *Sexual harassment: It's not academic.*)

Definitions of sexual harassment are important because they educate the campus community and workplace and promote discussion and conscientious evaluation of these experiences. They are also crucial to the process of helping those who have been harassed because most individuals do not identify what has happened to them as sexual harassment. In reference to academic sexual harassment, Crocker (1983) suggests, "The effectiveness of any definition will depend not only on the grievance procedure that enforces it, but also the commitment of the university administration and faculty to creating a truly nondiscriminatory environment for all students" (p. 707). MacKinnon (1979) notes that "it is not surprising . . . that women would not complain of an experience for which there has been no name. Until 1976, lacking a term to express it, sexual harassment was literally unspeakable, which made a generalized, shared, and social definition of it inaccessible" (p. 27). She further states that "the unnamed should not be taken for the nonexistent" (p. 28). (Current research indicates that two million women currently enrolled in undergraduate and graduate schools will experience some form of sexual harassment during their careers as students.)

Legal definitions

Two major types of definitions of sexual harassment have appeared in the legal, psychological, and educational literature. The first type includes legal and regulatory constructions and theoretical statements. Fitzgerald (1990) refers to these definitions as a priori definitions, theoretical in nature, which consist of a general statement describing the nature of the behavior. Table 1 presents a priori definitions from the Equal Employment Opportunity Commission (EEOC), the Office for Civil Rights (OCR) of the Department of Education, the National Advisory Council on Women's Educational Programs, and MacKinnon (1979).

Workplace and academic sexual harassment is clearly prohibited as a form of sexual discrimination, under both Title IX of the 1972 Education

---

TABLE 1. A Priori Definitions of Sexual Harassment

Equal Employment Opportunity Commission
Unwelcome sexual advances, requests for sexual favors, and other verbal or physical conduct of a sexual nature constitute sexual harassment when (1) submission to such conduct is made either explicitly or implicitly a term or condition of an individual's employment; (2) submission to, or rejection of, such conduct by an individual is used as the basis for employment decisions affecting such individual; or (3) such conduct has the purpose or effect of substantially interfering with an individual's work performance or creating an intimidating, hostile, or offensive working environment.

National Advisory Council on Women's Educational Programs
Academic sexual harassment is the use of authority to emphasize the sexuality or sexual identity of the student in a manner which prevents or impairs that student's full enjoyment of educational benefits, climate, or opportunities.

MacKinnon (1979)
Sexual harassment . . . refers to the unwanted impositions of sexual requirements in the context of a relationship of unequal power. Central to the concept is the use of power derived from one social sphere to lever benefits or impose deprivations in another. . . . When one is sexual, the other material, the cumulative sanction is particularly potent.

Office for Civil Rights, U.S. Department of Education
Sexual harassment consists of verbal or physical conduct of a sexual nature, imposed on the basis of sex, by an employee or agent of a recipient of federal funds that denies, limits, provides different, or conditions the provision of aid, benefits, services, or treatment protected under Title IX.

---

amendments and, for employees, Title VII of the 1964 Civil Rights Act. According to the EEOC's definition, the last condition—the creation of "an intimidating, hostile, or offensive working or learning environment"—is significant, because it covers the most pervasive form of sexual harassment, the form most often defended on the grounds of "academic freedom." In a 1986 decision, *Meritor Savings Bank v. Vinson*, the Supreme Court unanimously affirmed that "sexual harassment claims are not limited simply to those for which a tangible job benefit is withheld ["quid pro quo" sexual harassment], but also include those in which the complainant is subjected to an offensive, discriminatory work environment ("hostile environment" sexual harassment)" (Bennett-Alexander, 1987, p. 65). In doing so, the Court explicitly adopted the EEOC's guidelines, which have been extended to the academic community—especially to students, who are not covered by the statutes governing employer/employee relations—by the OCR. These guidelines thus have a regulating force supported by the U.S. Department of Education that is crucial to the effort to curtail the widespread sexual harassment now afflicting our colleges and universities.

In response to the decision in *Vinson,* and in the spirit of this effort, the American Council on Education issued the following statement to all its members in December 1986:

> Although the *Vinson* decision applies specifically to employment, it is prudent to examine the case and its implications for the campus setting. This provides an opportunity to renew institutional commitment to eliminating sexual harassment, or to develop an institution-wide program to address the problem. . . .

> The educational mission of a college or university is to foster an open learning and working environment. The ethical obligation to provide an environment that is free from sexual harassment and from the fear that it may occur is implicit. The entire collegiate community suffers when sexual harassment is allowed to pervade the academic atmosphere through neglect, the lack of a policy prohibiting it, or the lack of educational programs designed to clarify appropriate professional behavior on campus and to promote understanding of what constitutes sexual harassment. Each institution has the obligation, for moral as well as legal reasons, to develop policies, procedures, and programs that protect students and employees from sexual harassment and to establish an environment in which such unacceptable behavior will not be tolerated.

Empirical definitions

The second type of definition summarized by Fitzgerald (1990) is developed empirically, by investigating what various groups of individuals perceive sexual harassment to be under different circumstances (see table 2).

TABLE 2. Empirical Definitions of Sexual Harassment

Till (1980)
  Generalized sexist remarks
  Inappropriate and offensive, but essentially sanction-free sexual
    advances
  Solicitation of sexual activity or other sex-linked activity by promise
    of reward
  Coercion of sexual activity by threat of punishment
  Sexual crimes and misdemeanors

Fitzgerald et al. (1988)
  Gender harassment
  Seductive behavior
  Sexual bribery
  Sexual coercion
  Sexual imposition

The most useful definition is the one offered by Fitzgerald et al. (1988). They view sexual harassment along a continuum, with gender harassment on one end, and sexual imposition on the other. These levels correlate with legal definitions of sexual harassment. *Gender harassment* consists of generalized sexist remarks and behavior not designed to elicit sexual cooperation, but rather to convey insulting, degrading, or sexist attitudes about women or about lesbians and gays. *Seductive behavior* is unwanted, inappropriate, and offensive sexual advances. *Sexual bribery* is the solicitation of sexual activity or other sex-linked behavior by threat of punishment, *sexual coercion* is the coercion of sexual activity by threat of punishment, and *sexual imposition* includes gross sexual imposition, assault, and rape.

Based on her research with the measurement of sexual harassment, Fitzgerald (1990) offers the following definition:

> Sexual harassment consists of the sexualization of an instrumental relationship through the introduction or imposition of sexist or sexual remarks, requests, or requirements, in the context of a formal power differential. Harassment can also occur where no such formal power differential exists, if the behavior is unwanted by, or offensive to, the woman. Instances of harassment can be classified into the following general categories: gender harassment, seductive behavior, solicitation of sexual activity by promise of reward or threat of punishment, and sexual imposition or assault.

This definition has several advantages. First, it has an empirical component. Second, the nature and levels of sexual harassment are drawn from the experiences of women who have been so victimized. Third, the concept of intent is not addressed. It is, rather, the power differential and/or the woman's reaction that are considered to be the critical variables. As Fitzgerald (1990) states,

> When a formal power differential exists, all sexist or sexual behavior is seen as harassment, since the woman is not considered to be in a position to object, resist, or give fully free consent; when no such differential exists, it is the recipient's experience and perception of the behavior as offensive that constitutes the defining factor. (p 24)

We would add that the pervasive abuse and contempt for women and lesbians and gays in our culture underlie this form of harassment.

There is one issue that this definition does not specifically address: consensual relationships. The definition by Fitzgerald implies that consensual relationships are not possible within the context of unequal power and are inappropriate. As Zalk, Paludi, and Dederich (1990) point out with respect to academic sexual harassment:

> It is not just the distorted aggrandisement by the student or the greater store of knowledge that is granted the professor that frames the student's vision before and during the initial phases of the affair. The bottom line in the relationship is POWER. The faculty member has it and the student does not. As intertwined as the faculty-student roles may be, and as much as one must exist for the other to exist, they are not equal collaborators. The student does not negotiate, indeed, has nothing to negotiate with. There are no exceptions to this, and students know this.

Crocker (1983) argued that it is important to offer definitions of academic sexual harassment since

> they can educate the community and promote discussion and conscientious evaluation of behavior and experience. Students learn that certain experiences are officially recognized as wrong and punishable; professors are put on notice about behaviors that constitute sexual harassment; and administrators shape their understanding of the problem in a way that directs their actions on student inquiries and complaints. (p. 697)

Thus, a definition of academic sexual harassment sets the climate for the campus's response (as well as the workplace's response) to these incidents. Mead has called for "new taboos" against sexual harassment.

> What should we—what can we—do about sexual harassment on the job? . . . As I see it, it isn't more laws that we need now, but new taboos. . . .
>
> When we examine how any society works, it becomes clear that it is precisely the basic taboos—the deeply and intensely felt prohibitions against "unthinkable" behavior—that keep the social system in balance. . . . The complaints, the legal remedies, and the support institutions developed by women are all part of the response to the new conception of women's rights. But I believe we need something much more pervasive, a climate of opinion that includes men as well as women, and that will affect not only adult relations and behavior on the job but also the expectations about the adult world that guide our children's progress into that world. What we need, in fact, are new taboos, that are appropriate to the new society we are struggling to create—taboos that will operate within the work setting as once they operated within the household. Neither men nor women should expect that sex can be used either to victimize women who need to keep their jobs, or to keep women from advancement or to help men advance their own careers. (as quoted in Dziech & Weiner, 1984, p. 184)

Women Organized against Sexual Harassment (1981) at the University of California, Berkeley, proposed four requirements that have been used as guides by colleges and universities in writing their policy statements concerning sexual harassment. Guidelines must (1) acknowledge sexual harassment as sex discrimination, not as isolated instances of misconduct; (2) refer to a full range of harassment from subtle innuendoes to assault; (3) refer to ways in which the context of open and mutual academic exchange is polluted by harassment; and (4) refer to harassment as the imposition of sexual advances by a person in a position of authority. Crocker (1983) pointed out that to be effective, these requirements must (1) recognize the legal basis for university action and place the problem in a social context; (2) recognize the need for, and value of, specific examples that suggest the range of behaviors and experiences considered sexual harassment; (3) recognize the importance of sexual harassment for the integrity of the academy; and (4) recognize that sexual harassment occurs between people who have unequal power.

Workplace and academic sexual harassment is clearly prohibited as a form of sexual discrimination.

Defining academic sexual harassment from organizational and sociocultural power perspectives has been interpreted by some colleges and universities as including consensual relationships. Zacker and Paludi (1989) reported that some campuses have adopted a policy statement that includes information about consensual relationships (see table 3). Including consensual relationships as part of the definition of academic sexual harassment has been met with great resistance (Sandler, 1988; Zacker & Paludi, 1989). Men are much less likely than women to include consensual relationships in their definition of sexual harassment (Kenig & Ryan, 1986; Fitzgerald et al., 1988).

Incidence of sexual harassment

Table 4 summarizes the incidence rates of sexual harassment in the academic and workplace settings. As can be seen from this data, its occurrence in U.S. schools and business is widespread. Dziech and Weiner (1984) have reported that 30% of all undergraduate women suffer sexual harassment from at least one of their instructors during their college careers. When definitions of sexual harassment include sexist remarks and other forms of "gender harassment," the incidence rate in undergraduate populations nears 70% (Lott, Reilly, & Howard, 1982; Adams, Kottke, & Padgitt, 1983). These percentages translate into millions of students in our college system who are harassed each year. (According to the *Chroni-*

**TABLE 3. Policy Statements from Universities
that Deal with Consensual Relationships**

University of Iowa's Policy on Sexual Harassment
Amorous relationships between faculty members and students occurring outside the instructional context may lead to difficulties. Particularly when the faculty member and student are in the same academic unit or in units that are academically allied, relationships that the parties view as consensual may appear to others to be exploitative. Further, in such situations (and others that cannot be anticipated), the faculty member may face serious conflicts of interest and should be careful to distance himself or herself from any decisions that may reward or penalize the student involved. A faculty member who fails to withdraw from participation in activities or decisions that may reward or penalize a student with whom the faculty member has or has had an amorous relationship will be deemed to have violated his or her ethical obligation to the student, to other students, to colleagues, and to the University.

Harvard University's Policy on Sexual Harassment
Amorous relationships that might be appropriate in other circumstances are always wrong when they occur between any teacher or officer of the University and any student for whom he or she has a professional responsibility. Further, such relationships may have the effect of undermining the atmosphere of trust on which the educational process depends. Implicit in the idea of professionalism is the recognition by those in positions of authority that in their relationships with students there is always an element of power. It is incumbent upon those with authority not to abuse, nor to seem to abuse, the power with which they are entrusted. . . . Even when both parties have consented to the development of such a relationship, it is the officer or instructor who, by virtue of his or her special responsibility, will be held accountable for unprofessional behavior. Because graduate student teaching fellows, tutors, and undergraduate assistants may be less accustomed than faculty members to thinking of themselves as holding professional responsibilities, they would be wise to exercise special care in their relationships with students whom they instruct or evaluate. . . . Relationships between officers and students are always fundamentally asymmetric in nature.

cle of Higher Education, there were 6,835,900 women enrolled in under-graduate and graduate programs in 1987. Thirty percent of this figure equals more than 2,000,000 students who experience sexual harassment. When gender harassment is included, the number is 4,785,000.) The incidence rate for women graduate students and faculty is even higher (Bailey & Richards, 1985; Bond, 1988). Though there are few studies focusing on the harassment of nonfaculty employees in the college/university system, there is no reason to suppose that the harassment of college staff is any less than the 50% rate reported for employees of various other public and private institutions (Fitzgerald et al., 1988).

**TABLE 4. Summary of Research
on the Incidence of Sexual Harassment**

Adams, Kottke, and Padgitt (1983)
13% of women students surveyed reported they had avoided taking a class or working with certain professors because of the risk of being subjected to sexual advances; 17% received verbal sexual advances, 13.6% received sexual invitations; 6.4% had been subjected to physical advances; 2% received direct sexual assault

Chronicle of Higher Education Report of Harvard University (1983)
15% of the graduate students and 12% of the undergraduate students who had been sexually harassed by their professors changed their major or educational program because of the harassment

Wilson and Kraus (1983)
8.9% of the female undergraduates in their study had been pinched, touched, or patted to the point of personal discomfort

Bailey and Richards (1985)
12.7% of 246 graduate women surveyed reported that they had been sexually harassed; 21% had not enrolled in a course to avoid such behavior; 11.3% tried to report the behavior, 2.6% dropped a course because of it; 15.9% reported being directly assaulted

Bond (1988)
75% of 229 faculty experienced jokes with sexual themes during their graduate training; 68.9% were subjected to sexist comments demeaning to women; 57.8% of the women reported experiencing sexist remarks about their clothing, body, or sexual activities; 12.2% had unwanted intercourse, breast, or genital stimulation

Gutek (1985)
53.1% of private sector workers surveyed reported being fired, not being promoted, not given raises, all because of refusal to comply with requests for sexual relationships

Cornell University (Reported in Farley, 1978)
70% of 195 women workers reported sexual harassment and 56% of these women reported physical harassment

National Merit Systems Protection Board (1981)
42% of 23,000 women and men surveyed—the largest survey ever taken of workplace sexual harassment—experienced sexual harassment

While both women and men can be harassed, women make up the majority of victims. This is true for incidents of peer harassment as well. *Peer harassment* is the term used to describe the sexual harassment of women by their male colleagues—women students harassed by male students, for example; women faculty harassed by male faculty; and gay and lesbian students harassed by other students. Peer harassment includes all of the levels of sexual harassment: gender harassment, seductive behavior, sexual bribery, sexual coercion, and sexual imposition (see table 5).

Peer harassment occurs at all types of academic and business settings—large and small, private and public. Peer harassment creates an environment that makes education and work less than equal for women and men. There have been a few major surveys done on peer harassment. For example, in 1986, Cornell University surveyed its women students and found that 78% of those responding had experienced one or more forms of peer harassment, including sexist comments and unwelcome attention. While most of these experiences involved individual men, a substantial percentage involved groups of men, termed *group harassment*. MIT also conducted a study of peer harassment and reported that 92% of the women were harassed by male students. At the University of Rhode Island, 70% of the women reported instances of peer harassment.

TABLE 5. Illustrations of Peer Harassment

A group of men regularly sit at a table facing a cafeteria line. As women go through the line, the men loudly discuss the women's sexual attributes and hold up signs with numbers from 1 to 10, "rating" each woman. As a result, many women skip meals or avoid the cafeteria.

Sexist posters and pictures appear in places where women will see them.

A fraternity pledge approaches a young woman he has never met and bites her on the breast—a practice called "sharking."

A particular shop [class's] predominantly male population designated one shop day as "National Sexual Harassment Day," in honor of their only female student. They gave her nonstop harassment throughout the day, and found it to be so successful (the female student [dropped the course]) that they later held a "National Sexual Harassment Week."

Source: Project on the Status and Education of Women.

These surveys also indicate that the most serious forms of peer harassment involve groups of men. When men outnumber women, as in fraternity houses, stadiums, and parties, group harassment is especially likely to occur. Examples of group harassment include:

"scoping," which involves rating women's attractiveness on a scale from 1 to 10;

yelling, whistling, and shouting obscenities at women who walk by fraternity houses or other campus sites;

intimidating a woman by surrounding her, demanding that she expose her breasts, and not allowing her to leave until she complies;

creating a disturbance outside of women's residence halls;

vandalizing sororities;

harassing women who support women's rights;

date rape.

Research has indicated that while any individual is likely to be sexually harassed, women tend to experience this more often than others. Sandler (1988) and DeFour (1990) have indicated that on many campuses ethnic minority women are victims because of the stereotypes and myths that portray them as sexually active, exotic, and erotic. There is thus an interface of racism and sexism in some elements of sexual harassment.

Definitions of sexual harassment are important because they educate the campus community.

In addition, physically challenged women experience a considerable amount of psychological victimization when reporting sexual harassment due to stereotypes about their sexuality and attractiveness. Lesbians and gays have been the victims of gender harassment and other forms of sexual harassment because of homophobic attitudes. Individuals who support women's studies programs and are feminists are also often targeted.

Most of the current incidence rates of sexual harassment have been obtained from research using the Sexual Experiences Questionnaire (Fitzgerald & Shullman, 1985). All of the items in the survey are written in behavioral terms and take the form of: "Have you ever been in a situation where a professor or instructor . . . ?" The term *sexual harassment* does not appear in any item until the end ("Have you ever been sexually harassed by a professor or instructor?"). Items represent the five levels of sexual harassment derived from research: gender harassment, seductive behavior, sexual bribery, sexual coercion, and sexual assault. For each item, individuals are asked to circle the response most closely describing their own experiences: "Never," "Once," and "More than Once." If individuals indicate that the behavior has happened either once or more than once, they are further instructed to identify the sex of the faculty member: "Male," "Female," or "Both Male and Female." Information concerning the reliability and validity of this instrument and parallel forms for employees may be found in Fitzgerald et al. (1988).

Research with this instrument has indicated that women are more likely to be the recipients of sexual harassment than men. In nearly all cases, the perpetrators are men. Furthermore, while the majority of women in undergraduate and graduate training programs as well as in the workplace indicate that they have experienced behaviors that legally constitute sexual harassment, they fail to recognize and label their experiences as such. For example, Fitzgerald et al. (1988) found that although at one university nearly 28% of the women administrators reported that they had been propositioned by male co-workers, only 5% of the women felt that they had been sexually harassed.

Fitzgerald and Weitzman (1990) reported that of the 235 male faculty members they surveyed (using a modified form of the Sexual Experiences Questionnaire), the majority reported engaging in behavior that meets the legal definition of sexual harassment, yet only one man reported that he had sexually harassed a student. Fitzgerald and Weitzman further concluded that faculty who sexually harass students are not distinguishable from their colleagues with respect to age, marital status, academic rank, or academic discipline. Sexual harassers tend to be repeat offenders, however.

Different conclusions were drawn from research conducted by the United States Merit Systems Protection Board (1981). Surveys were sent to more than 23,000 women and men civilian employees of the Executive Branch of the U.S. government; a response rate of 85% was achieved. Results indicated that women in the federal workforce are likely to be harassed by a male co-worker who is married, older than the woman, and white, and who harassed other women as well. Results also indicated that when the harassment involved attempted rape or sexual assault, supervisors were more likely to be the harasser of the women than were peers.

Do women harass?

Research in academic sexual harassment suggests that women professors are highly unlikely to date or initiate sexual relationships with male or female students (Fitzgerald & Weitzman, 1990). In the workplace as in the academic environment, women are much less likely to hold the organizational power that would permit them to offer sexual rewards and/or punishments. As Fitzgerald and Weitzman conclude:

> Although it is theoretically possible for women to harass men, it is, in practice, an extremely rare event. This is due both to the women's relative lack of formal power, and the socialization that stigmatizes the sexually aggressive woman. Reports by male subjects of sexual overtures by women co-workers not only do not constitute harassment in any formal sense, but must also be evaluated in light of data suggesting that men are likely to interpret relatively innocuous behavior as invitations to sexual contact. (p. 66)

Taking action

Both formal academic research and the growing experience of those taking action against harassment in the campus community and workplace indicate that it is one of the most pervasive and least recognized forms of abuse in our society. In the 1981 study by the National Merit Systems Protection Board, of over 23,000 employees, 42% reported harassment. Numerous studies have produced similar (and higher) rates for students in undergraduate and graduate institutions. Based on enrollment figures for 1987, reported in the *Chronicle of Higher Education*, over 2,000,000 undergraduate and graduate women students will be singled out for harassment during their academic careers. When gender harassment is added to the continuum of sexual harassment, the number nearly doubles.

Sexual harassment is clearly prohibited as a form of discrimination under Title IX of the 1972 Education amendments and Title VII of the 1964 Civil Rights Act. Despite these federal statutes, only a few colleges, businesses, and agencies have implemented active programs in order to educate their constituents and to investigate complaints. Because both harassers and the harassed usually fail to identify the abuse as sexual harassment, most incidents go unreported even when a mechanism for redress exists. Those seeking to reduce the incidence of sexual harassment in campus environments have found that an intensive educational campaign is a precondition for success.

Because of power structures within the workplace and the academy and because of deeply embedded cultural biases, women are overwhelmingly the targets of sexual harassment. And even though no "profile" of a typical harasser has been developed in research, nearly all harassers are male. Identification of sexual harassment as a "women's issue," however, rather than as a pervasive pattern of abuse that contaminates a whole community, only creates another impediment to its identification and elimination.

Notes

Sample References on Workplace Sexual Harassment

Bennett-Alexander, D.D. (1987). The Supreme Court finally speaks on the issue of sexual harassment—what did it say? *Women's Rights Law Reporter, 10*, 65-78.

Farley, L. (1978). *Sexual shakedown: The sexual harassment of women on the job.* New York: McGraw-Hill.

Goodwin, M.P., Roscoe, B., Rose, M., & Repp, S.E. (1989). Sexual harassment: Experiences of university employees. *Initiatives, 52*, 25-33.

Gruber, J., & Bjorn, L. (1982). Blue-collar blues: The sexual harassment of women autoworkers. *Work and Occupations: An International Sociological Journal, 9*, 271–98.

Gutek, B. (1985) *Sex and the workplace: The impact of sexual behavior and harassment on women, men, and organizations.* San Francisco: Jossey-Bass.

Gutek, B., & Dunwoody, V. (1987). Understanding sex in the workplace. *Women and Work, 2*, 249–69.

Hair, S. (1987). Sexual harassment, subtle or overt gnaws at productivity. *Employee Assistance Quarterly, 3*, 67–70.

Hopkins, C., & Johnson, D.A. (1982). Sexual harassment in the workplace. *Journal of College Placement, 42*, 30–35.

Lafontaine, E., & Treadeau, L. (1986). The frequency, sources, and correlates of sexual harassment among women in traditional male occupations. *Sex Roles, 15*, 433–42.

Littler-Bishop, S., Seidler-Feller, D., & Opaluch, R. (1982). Sexual harassment in the workplace as a function of initiator's status: The case of airline personnel. *The Journal of Social Issues, 38*, 137–48.

Loy, P., & Stewart, L. (1984). The extent and effects of the sexual harassment of working women. *Sociological Focus, 17*, 31–43.

MacKinnon, C. (1979). *Sexual harassment of working women: A case of sex discrimination.* New Haven, Conn.: Yale University Press.

Maypole, D. (1986). Sexual harassment of social workers at work: Injustice within? *Social Work, 31*, 29–34.

Maypole, D., & Skaine, R. (1983). Sexual harassment in the workplace. *Social Work, 28*, 385–90.

Petersen, D., & Massengill, D. (1982). Sexual harassment: A growing problem in the workplace. *Personnel Administrator, 27*, 79–89.

Popovich, P. (1988). Sexual harassment in organizations. *Employee Responsibilities and Rights Journal, 1*, 273–82.

United States Merit Systems Protection Board (1981). *Sexual harassment in the federal workplace: Is it a problem?* Washington, D.C.: U.S. Government Printing Office.

Sample References on Academic Sexual Harassment

Adams, J. Kottke, J., & Padgitt, J. (1983). Sexual harassment of university students. *Journal of College Student Personnel, 24,* 484–90.

Association of American Colleges (1988). *Peer harassment: Hassles for women on campus.* Washington, D.C.: Project on the Status and Education of Women.

Bailey, N., & Richards, M. (1985, August). *Tarnishing the ivory tower: Sexual harassment in graduate training programs.* Paper presented at the Annual Meeting of the American Psychological Association, Los Angeles, CA.

Betts, N., & Newman, G. (1982). Defining the issues: Sexual harassment in college and university life. *Contemporary Education, 54,* 48–52.

Bond, M. (1988). Division 27 Sexual harassment survey: Definition, impact, and environmental context. *The Community Psychologist, 21,* 7–10.

Cammaert, L. (1985). How widespread is sexual harassment on campus? Special Issue: Women in groups and aggression against women. *International Journal of Women's Studies, 8,* 388–97.

Coleman, M. (1987). A study of sexual harassment of female students in academia. *Dissertation Abstracts International, 47,* 2815.

Connolly, W.B., Jr., & Marshall, A.B. (1989). Sexual harassment of university or college students by faculty members. *Journal of College and University Law, 15,* 381–403.

Crocker, P. (1983). An analysis of university definitions of sexual harassment. *Signs, 8,* 696–707.

DeFour, D.C. (1990). The interface of racism and sexism on college campuses. In M.A. Paludi (Ed.), *Ivory power: Sexual harassment on campus.* Albany: SUNY Press.

Dziech, B., & Weiner, L. (1984). *The lecherous professor.* Boston: Beacon Press.

Fitzgerald, L.F. (1990). Sexual harassment: The definition and measurement of a construct. In M.A. Paludi (Ed.), *Ivory power: Sexual harassment on campus.* Albany: SUNY Press.

Fitzgerald, L.F., & Shullman, S. (1985, August). The development and validation of an objectively scored measure of sexual harassment. Paper presented at the Annual Meeting of the American Psychological Association, Los Angeles.

Fitzgerald, L., Shullman, S., Bailey, N., Richards, M., Swecker, J., Gold, Y., Ormerod, M., & Weitzman, L. (1988). The incidence and dimensions of sexual harassment in academia and the workplace. *Journal of Vocational Behavior, 32,* 152–75.

Fitzgerald, L.F., & Weitzman, L. (1990). Men who harass: Speculation and data. In M.A. Paludi (Ed.), *Ivory power: Sexual harassment on campus.* Albany: SUNY Press.

Franklin, P., Moglin, H., Zatling-Boring, P., & Angress, R. (1981). *Sexual and gender harassment in the academy.* New York: Modern Language Association.

Gartland, P. (Ed.) (1983). Sexual harassment on campus. *Journal of the National Association of Women Deans, Administrators and Counselors, 46,* 3–50.

Ingulli, E.D. (1987). Sexual harassment in education. *Rutgers Law Journal, 18,* 281–342.

Kenig, S., & Ryan, J. (1986). Sex differences in levels of tolerance and attribution of blame for sexual harassment on a university campus. *Sex Roles, 15,* 535–49.

Lott, B. (1982). Sexual assault and harassment: A campus community case study. *Signs, 8,* 296–319.

Lott, B., Reilly, M.E., & Howard, D.R. (1982). Sexual assault and harassment: A campus community case study. *Signs, 8,* 296–319.

Mazer, D.B., & Percival, E.F. (1989). Students' experiences of sexual harassment at a small university. *Sex Roles, 20,* 1–22.

Reilly, M., Lott, B., & Gallogly, S. (1986). Sexual harassment of university students. *Sex Roles, 15,* 333–58.

Robertson, C. (1988). Campus harassment: Sexual harassment policies and procedures at institutions of higher learning. *Signs, 13,* 792–812.

Sandler, B. (1981). Sexual harassment: A hidden problem. *Educational Record, 62,* 52–57.

Sandler, B. (1988, April). Sexual harassment: A new issue for institutions, or these are the times that try men's souls. Paper presented at the Conference on Sexual Harassment on Campus, New York.

Schneider, B. (1987). Graduate women, sexual harassment, and university policy. *Journal of Higher Education, 58,* 46–65.

Singer, T.L. (1989). Sexual harassment in graduate schools of social work: Provocative dilemmas. *Journal of Social Work Education, 25,* 68–76.

Small, M.J. (1989). The guardians of Heloise? Sexual harassment in higher education. *Educational Record, 70,* 42–45.

Somers, A. (1982). Sexual harassment in academe: Legal issues and definitions. *The Journal of Social Issues, 38,* 23–32.

Till, F. (1980). *Sexual harassment: A report on the sexual harassment of students.* Washington, D.C.: National Advisory Council on Women's Educational Programs.

Wilson, K.R., & Krauss, L.A. (1983). Sexual harassment in the university. *Journal of College Student Personnel, 24,* 219–24.

Zacker, M., & Paludi, M.A. (1989). Educational programs for academic sexual harassment. Unpublished manuscript, Hunter College.

Zalk, S.R., Paludi, M.A., & Dederich, J. (1990). Women students' assessment of consensual relationships with their professors. Manuscript in preparation, Hunter College.

6

Legal Definitions of Sexual Harassment Must Be Broad

Deborah L. Siegel

Deborah L. Siegel compiled and wrote the report Sexual Harassment: Research and Resources *for the National Council for Research on Women (NCRW). NCRW is a coalition of centers and organizations that conduct feminist research, policy analysis, and educational programs.*

Men and women often see sexualized behavior differently, in part because women are more likely to be sexually assaulted. There is often a major difference between the intent (the man's) and the impact (on the woman). Sexual harassment is one such gray area, especially since sexual harassment is part of a spectrum of victimization ranging from leering to rape. Gender-based differences in interpretation are most likely in "hostile environment" cases that do not involve physical assault or quid pro quo demands. The Equal Employment Opportunity Commission and the Supreme Court have responded to these gray areas of interpretation by setting forth clear, broad definitions of sexual harassment that recognize the impact of such behavior on a "reasonable woman." Unfortunately, although the legal definitions are being refined, many people still operate under sexual myths and stereotypes that blame the victim and downplay the severity of sexual harassment.

"The unnamed should not be taken for the nonexistent" (MacKinnon 1979, p. 28).

Until recently, few people openly discussed sexual harassment. And as Louise Fitzgerald, a psychologist at the University of Illinois at Champaign-Urbana, points out, we still lack a common definition (Fitzgerald, 1990). The first federal statute prohibiting sex discrimination in the workplace was not passed until the 1960s; the phrase *sexual harassment* was not coined until the mid-1970s; and the U.S. Supreme Court did not recognize sexual harassment until 1986.

"It is not surprising . . . that women would not complain of an experience for which there has been no name. Until 1976, lacking a term to express it, sexual harassment was literally unspeakable, which made generalized, shared and social definitions of it inaccessible" (MacKinnon 1979, p. 27).

Deborah L. Siegel, *Sexual Harassment: Research and Resources*, published by the National Council for Research on Women, ©1991. All rights reserved. Reprinted with permission.

Originally thought to be limited to those relatively rare situations where women are compelled to trade sexual favors for professional survival (known as *quid pro quo*), sexual harassment is now recognized more broadly as "the inappropriate sexualization of an otherwise nonsexual relationship, an assertion by men of the primacy of a woman's sexuality over her role as worker, [professional colleague,] or student" (Fitzgerald and Ormerod 1991a, p. 2).

Because women are much more likely to be victims of rape and sexual assault, women have a "stronger incentive to be concerned with sexual behavior."

Legal scholars like Catharine MacKinnon, a professor at the School of Law, University of Michigan, and activists like Susan Brownmiller are credited with initiating the view of sexual harassment that has radically changed the way sexual harassment complaints are treated under the legal system. Shifting the focus of sexual harassment from the belief that males' sexual pursuit of women in the workplace or the classroom is essentially biological and that sexual harassment is therefore a "normal" consequence of attraction between the sexes, MacKinnon, Brownmiller, and others advocate a "dominance" approach. In *The Sexual Harassment of Working Women* (1979), MacKinnon claims that "sexual harassment, most broadly defined, refers to the unwanted imposition of sexual requirements in the context of a relationship of unequal power" (p. 1). Based on her analysis of legal cases and her examination of sexual harassment as women report experiencing it, MacKinnon explains why sexual harassment *is* sex discrimination. It occurs in the workplace because women occupy largely inferior job positions and roles. At the same time it also works to keep women "in their place."

Legal definitions
"The law sees and treats women the way men see and treat women" (MacKinnon 1979, p. 40).

The first litigation of sexual harassment claims did not occur until the mid-seventies. Title VII of the 1964 Civil Rights Act prohibiting sex discrimination in the workplace was followed eight years later by Title IX of the 1972 Higher Education Amendments prohibiting sex discrimination in educational institutions receiving federal assistance. But in much of the early adjudication of sex discrimination, the phenomenon of sexual harassment was typically seen "as isolated and idiosyncratic, or as natural and universal, and, in either case, as inappropriate for legal intervention" (Rhode 1989, p. 233). It was not until 1980 that the Equal Employment Opportunity Commission, in its "Guidelines on Discrimination," explicitly defined sexual harassment under Title VII as a form of unlawful, sex-based discrimination. In 1984, the guidelines were expanded to include educational institutions. According to the 1984 EEOC "Policy Statement on Sexual Harassment,"

> Unwelcome sexual advances, requests for sexual favors, and other verbal or physical conduct of a sexual nature constitutes sexual harassment when

(1) submission to such conduct is made either explicitly or implicitly a term or condition of an individual's employment or academic advancement,

(2) submission to or rejection of such conduct by an individual is used as the basis for employment decisions or academic decisions affecting such individual, or

(3) such conduct has the purpose or effect of unreasonably interfering with an individual's work or academic performance or creating an intimidating, hostile, or offensive working or academic environment.

In 1986, the Supreme Court, in a unanimous decision in *Meritor Savings Bank, FSB v. Vinson*, upheld this interpretation of Title VII and the EEOC guidelines that define as prohibited discrimination the existence of a hostile or threatening work environment. Rejecting the contention that Title VII prohibits only discrimination that causes tangible economic harm, the Court ruled instead that under Title VII employees have the right to work in environments free from discriminatory intimidation, ridicule, and insult (477 U.S.57 1986).

The law does make a distinction between *quid pro quo* cases that fall under Section (2) of the EEOC guidelines, in which the harassment involves trading sex for work, and cases that fall under Section (3), "hostile environment" or what MacKinnon calls "conditions of work" harassment, in which unwanted and offensive sexual behavior is present in the workplace but not attached to job-related financial detriment or reward.

While the language and terms of Sections (1) and (2) of the EEOC guidelines are clear, the language in Section (3) defining a "hostile environment" has allowed considerable latitude for interpretation, continuing to cause confusion and ambiguity both in and out of the courts. Comments such as, "Can't you take a joke?" "You're being overly sensitive," and "Lighten up!" are painfully familiar to any woman who has experienced the humiliation of sexual harassment. In all cases, the burden of proof for sexual harassment and "hostile environment" falls entirely on the accuser. Says Stephanie Riger, Professor of Sociology at the University of Illinois, Champaign-Urbana, "Courts have required that incidents falling into [Section (3)] . . . be repeated in order to establish that such an environment exists; these incidents must be both pervasive and so severe that they affect the victim's psychological well-being" (Riger 1991, p. 498).

Victims' rights to collect damages continue to be limited under federal law. While the 1991 Civil Rights Act, which recently passed the Senate, does not limit awards for back pay and past out-of-pocket damages like medical bills, the compromise forged to ensure passage of the bill in Congress and gain White House approval limits other damages according to the size of the employer's work force. Unlike the potential damages available to victims of racial discrimination, damages for sex discrimination are capped at $50,000 for small companies and $300,000 for larger ones.

The "reasonable person" rule

As the law has been interpreted, prohibition against sexual harassment in the workplace technically covers any remark or behavior that is sufficiently severe and pervasive that not only the victim's but also a "reasonable person's" psychological well-being would be affected. But a 1991 landmark ruling by the Court of Appeals for the Ninth Circuit in California held that "the appropriate perspective for judging a hostile environment claim is that of the 'reasonable woman' and recognized that a woman's perspective may differ substantially from a man's" (Estrich 1991). In his ruling, Judge Robert Beezer observed, "Conduct that many men consider unobjectionable may offend many women." Because women are much more likely to be victims of rape and sexual assault, women have a "stronger incentive to be concerned with sexual behavior." Michele Paludi, Professor of Psychology at Hunter College, City University of New York, points out there may also be "a difference between intent and impact. Many [men] may not intend it, but some things they do may be experienced by women as sexual harassment. A touch or comment can be seen very differently" (Goleman 1991, p. C12).

Gender has clearly proven to be the most influential factor in determining whether incidents will be defined as sexual harassment.

While the 1991 Ninth Circuit Court ruling acknowledges that men and women may interpret the same behavior differently, in application this legal understanding is often overshadowed by a grave misunderstanding of the nature of sexual harassment as experienced by its victims. Says Susan Estrich, Professor of Law at University of Southern California, "The people doing the judging are in no position to understand the position of those being judged. The powerful make judgments against the powerless" (conversation with the National Council for Research on Women, October 25, 1991).

Stephanie Riger notes that "the dilemma in applying [the 'reasonable person' standard] to sexual harassment is that a reasonable woman and a reasonable man are likely to differ in their judgment of what is offensive." And Riger adds, "Men's judgments about what behavior constitutes harassment, and who is to blame, are likely to prevail" (Riger 1991, p. 498, 499). Deborah Rhode, Professor of Law at Stanford Law School, points out that in terms of the court, what constitutes harassment—and what determines the amounts of awards for damages under state law and in the future under federal law—"ultimately depends on the perceptions of the judge rather than the victim, and the vestiges of long-standing prejudices do not seem entirely absent from judicial as well as workplace forums" (Rhode 1989, p. 235).

Research-based definitions

As a result of such legal gray areas, researchers have constructed more explicit definitions based on sexual harassment as women report experiencing it. Sexually harassing behavior falls into categories, differing in severity. Such definitions aim for clearer understanding of what constitutes a "hostile environment." One of the most widely used models breaks harassing behavior into five basic types of sexual harassment:

Five Types of Sexual Harassment

Type 1:   Gender Harassment
          generalized sexist remarks and behavior

Type 2:   Seductive Behavior
          inappropriate and offensive but essentially sanction-free behavior, with
          no penalty attached to noncompliance
Type 3:   Sexual Bribery
          solicitation of sexual activity or other sex-linked behavior by promise of
          rewards
Type 4:   Sexual Coercion
          coercion of sexual activity by threat of punishment
Type 5:   Sexual Imposition or Assault
          gross sexual imposition like touching, fondling, grabbing, or assault
          (Till 1980).

Researchers agree that women link different kinds of sexualized behavior in the workplace in ways that men, on the average, do not. Says Mary Rowe, Special Assistant to the President at Massachusetts Institute of Technology, "Mild sexualized behavior such as flirting or joking is often seen as sexualized by the woman and not by the man" (conversation with National Council for Research on Women, October 24, 1991).

Research literature documenting perceptions of sexual harassment—by whom and when a particular behavior will be interpreted as sexual harassment—is fairly well developed (Fitzgerald and Ormerod 1991a). Variables analyzed include the gender of the perceiver, severity and explicitness of the behavior, status of the initiator, degree of power in the relationship between the individuals involved, behavior of the victim, and attitudes of the perceiver (most notably attitudes about feminism). In all the studies, gender has clearly proven to be the most influential factor in determining whether incidents will be defined as sexual harassment, with women universally more likely to label a given situation as harassing than men (Collins and Blodgett 1981; Lazarus and Folkman 1984; Gutek 1985; Padgitt 1986; Powell 1986; Fitzgerald and Ormerod 1991b).

When college men and women were presented with hypothetical scenarios, for example, women spotted harassment at much earlier stages. In one scenario, a male department chair invites a new female employee to lunch to discuss her work. He focuses the lunchtime conversation on her personal life. On another occasion, over drinks, he tries to fondle her. "Most of the women said that sexual harassment started at the first lunch, when he talked about her private life instead of her work. Most of the men said that sexual harassment began at the point he fondled her" (Paludi 1991a).

In a study conducted by Barbara Gutek, 67% of men surveyed said they would be complimented if they were propositioned by a woman at work. Only 17% of women said they would take such a proposition as a compliment (Goleman 1991, p. C12).

Women's definitions

Most women who are sexually harassed never say anything. In the 1987 U.S. Merit Systems Protection Board survey of federal employees, only 5% of those who indicated they had experienced sexual harassment actually filed formal complaints or requested investigations. Experts on the issue agree that the overwhelming majority of sexual harassment goes unreported. "In most organizations, at least 90% of sexual harassment victims are unwilling to come forward for two reasons: fear of retaliation and fear of loss of privacy" (Klein 1991).

Regardless of whether they formally voice a complaint, when *do* women say it is a problem? According to Claire Safran, in her survey for *Redbook* magazine in 1976, "Objection to sexual harassment at work is not a neopuritan moral protest against signs of attraction, displays of affection, compliments, flirtation, or touching on the job. Instead, women are rattled and often angry about sex that is one-sided, unwelcome, or comes with strings attached. When it's something a woman wants to turn off but can't (a co-worker or supervisor who refuses to stop) or when it's coming from someone with the economic power to hire or fire, help or hinder, reward or punish (an employer or client who mustn't be offended)—that's when [women] say it's a problem" (Safran 1976).

Sexual harassment . . . is the most recent form of victimization of women to be redefined as a social rather than a personal problem, following rape and wife abuse.

The resignation of one of the nation's first female neurosurgeons from her senior faculty position at Stanford Medical School dramatized one woman's saying "it's a problem." Dr. Frances Conley reported that her male colleagues called her "honey" in the operating room and fondled her legs under the table. Stanford medical students also reported that slides of *Playboy* centerfolds were still being used to "spice up" lectures. Although Dr. Conley has since resumed her position, when asked what finally made her quit, she noted that the problems had not lessened in more than 20 years and a colleague who was seen as responsible for harassing was promoted to a senior administrative post at the medical school. "I had not realized how pervasive the sexism was," Conley responded. "I couldn't brush it off. I couldn't pretend to be one of the boys any longer" (*The New York Times*, June 4, 1991).

Sexual harassment and violence against women

"Sexual harassment . . . is the most recent form of victimization of women to be redefined as a social rather than a personal problem, following rape and wife abuse" (Riger 1991, p. 497).

Susan Estrich examines similarities between the doctrines of rape law and the legal tools used in sexual harassment cases: "The rules and prejudices have been borrowed almost wholesale from traditional rape law. The focus on the conduct of the woman—her reactions or lack of them, her resistance or lack of it—reappears with only the most minor changes" (Estrich 1991, p. 815). Estrich's analysis of the rulings that have shaped sexual harassment law illuminates the durability of sexism in the law's judgment of the sexual relations of men and women.

There are *"many similarities between sexual harassment and other forms of sexual victimization, not only in the secrecy that surrounds them but in the mythology that supports them" (Fitzgerald and Ormerod 1991a, p. 2).*

Like rape, sexual harassment is not an issue of lust; it is an issue of power. Sexual harassment *must* be seen as part of a continuum of sexual victimization that ranges from staring and leering to assault and rape (Bunch 1991). "Most sexual harassment starts at the subtle end of the continuum and escalates over time. Each year, 1% of women in the U.S. labor force are sexually assaulted on the job" (Klein 1991). Yet cultural mythologies consistently blame the victim for sexual abuse and act to keep women "in their place" (MacKinnon 1979; Copeland and Wolfe 1991). Scholars have identified several similarities in attitudes toward rape and sexual harassment, essentially revealing cultural myths that blame the victim:

1. *Women ask for it*

Rape: Victims "seduce" their rapists.

Sexual Harassment: Sexual harassment is a form of seduction; women precipitate harassment by the way they dress and talk.

2. *Women say no but mean yes*

Rape: Women secretly need and want to be forced into sex. They don't know what they want.

Sexual Harassment: Women like the attention. Harassment usually continues or escalates when the victim has given no positive response or a negative response. Harassers offer such excuses as "I know her better than she knows herself."

3. *Women lie*

Rape: In most charges of "rape," the woman is lying.

Sexual Harassment: Women lie about sexual harassment in order to get men they dislike in trouble (Quina 1990, p. 96).

Perhaps the most dangerous of these myths is the assumption that since women seem to "go along" with sexual harassment, they must like it, which means that sexual harassment is not really harassment at all. But as researcher Lynn Wehrli points out, "This constitutes more than a simplistic denial of all we know about the ways in which socialization and economic dependence foster submissiveness and override free choice. . . . Those women who are able to speak out about sexual harassment use terms such as *humiliating, intimidating, frightening, financially damaging, embarrassing, nerve-wracking, awful,* and *frustrating.* . . . These are hardly words used to describe a situation which one 'likes'" (MacKinnon 1979, p. 48).

Notes

Brownmiller, Susan. 1975. *Against Our Will: Men, Women, and Rape.* New York: Simon & Schuster.

Bunch, Charlotte, 1991. "Women's Rights As Human Rights: Toward a Re-Vision of Human Rights." In *Gender Violence: A Development and Human Rights Issue.* New Brunswick, NJ: Center for Women's Global Leadership, Rutgers University.

Collins, E.G., and T.B. Blodgitt. 1981. "Sexual Harassment: Some See It . . . Some Won't," *Harvard Business Review,* Vol. 59, 76-95.

Copeland, Lois, and Leslie R. Wolfe. 1991. *Violence Against Women as Bias Motivated Hate Crime: Defining the Issues.* Washington, DC: Center for

Women Policy Studies.

Estrich, Susan. 1991, April. "Sex at Work," *Stanford Law Review*, Vol. 43, 813.

Fitzgerald, Louise F. 1990. "Sexual Harassment: The Definition and Measurement of a Construct." In M. Paludi, Ed., *Ivory Power: Sexual Harassment on Campus*. Albany: State University of New York Press.

Fitzgerald, Louise F., and A.J. Ormerod. 1991a, in press. "Breaking Silence: The Sexual Harassment of Women in Academia and the Workplace." Chapter to appear in F. Denmark and M. Paludi, Eds., *Handbook of the Psychology of Women*. New York: Greenwood Press.

Fitzgerald, Louise F., and A.J. Ormerod. 1991b. "Perceptions of Sexual Harassment: The Influence of Gender and Context," *Psychology of Women Quarterly*, Vol. 15, 281-294.

Goleman, Daniel. 1991. "Sexual Harassment: It's About Power, Not Lust," *The New York Times*, October 22, 1991, C1, C12.

Gutek, Barbara, 1985. *Sex and the Workplace*. San Francisco: Jossey-Bass.

Klein, Freada. 1991. Testimony before the Committee on Education and Labor, House of Representatives, Hearings on H.R.1, the Civil Rights Act of 1991.

Lazarus, R.S., and S. Folkman. 1984. *Stress, Appraisal and Coping*. New York: Springer.

MacKinnon, Catharine. 1979. *Sexual Harassment of Working Women*. New Haven, Yale University Press.

The New York Times. 1991, June 4. "Citing Sexism, Stanford Doctor Quits," C16.

Padgitt, S.C., and J.S. Padgitt. 1986. "Cognitive Structure of Sexual Harassment: Implications for University Policy," *Journal of College Student Personnel*, Vol. 27, 34-39.

Paludi, Michele. 1991a, August. "Education and Training in Sexual Harassment on Campus." Presentation at the American Psychological Association, San Francisco.

Paludi, Michele, Ed. 1991b. *Working 9 to 5: Women, Men, Sex, and Power*. Albany: State University of New York Press.

Powell, G.N. 1986. "Effects of Sex-Role Identity and Sex on Definitions of Sexual Harassment," *Sex Roles*, Vol. 14, 9-19.

Quina, Kathryn. 1990. "The Victimizations of Women." In M. Paludi, Ed., *Ivory Power: Sexual Harassment on Campus*. Albany: State University of New York Press.

Rhode, Deborah. 1989. *Justice and Gender: Sex Discrimination and Law*. Cambridge: Harvard University Press.

Riger, Stephanie. 1991. "Gender Dilemmas in Sexual Harassment Policies and Procedures," *American Psychologist*, Vol. 46:5, 497-505.

Safran, Claire. 1976, November. "What Men Do to Women on the Job: A Shocking Look at Sexual Harassment," *Redbook*, 149, 217-223.

Till, F.J. 1980. *Sexual Harassment: A Report on the Sexual Harassment of Students*. Washington, DC: National Advisory Council on Women's Educational Programs.

Wehrli, Lynn. 1976. *Sexual Harassment at the Workplace: A Feminist Analysis and Strategy for Change*. M.A. Thesis, Massachusetts Institute of Technology.

7

Current Legal Definitions of Sexual Harassment Are Too Broad

Lloyd R. Cohen

Lloyd R. Cohen is associate professor of law at Chicago-Kent College of Law. He has written and lectured extensively on ethics and law.

Current legal definitions of sexual harassment are too broad. Sexual harassment cases are simply attempts to enforce rigid moral codes using the court system. By using broader definitions of sexual harassment than the rest of society, the courts send the message that much of the ordinary social interaction between men and women will be strictly regulated, chilling relations between the sexes.

At the mention of the term sexual harassment, I feel the intellectual ground give way beneath my feet. Sexual harassment is a term that has, like fascist and racist, some intellectual content and strong pejorative implication, but lacks a clear definition. As in the case of the other two terms, it is not by accident that the definition of sexual harassment has become more, rather than less, elusive with use.

The problem is not simply that the ordinary language meaning of the phrase is insufficiently narrow and precise to capture the activities it is meant to cover. Another important source of difficulty is that, as with many politicized phrases, sexual harassment is deliberately employed loosely and imprecisely. The term connotes a social and legal wrong, and invites being employed as a broad brush to tar behavior to which a speaker objects even if the audience might not. Sexual banter, displaying *Playboy* centerfolds, requests for sex in exchange for job promotions, and rape can all be lumped together as sexual harassment. If the label sticks, the former acts will be tainted by the latter.

It makes a thoughtful person uneasy when a term that is intended to have moral, social, and legal consequences is bandied about without an implicit or explicit definition. When someone uses the term sexual harassment, it is unclear (1) what class of behavior the speaker implicitly wishes to condemn; and (2) what social and legal consequences are ex-

Lloyd R. Cohen, "Sexual Harassment and the Law," *Society*, May/June 1991. Copyright ©1991 by Transaction Publishers. Reprinted with permission.

pected to flow from that condemnation. While some forms of sexual harassment need to be punished and stigmatized, I distrust the use of a category that seems too broad at both ends. Rape, sexual assault, and obscene phone calls could all be described as sexual harassment. But to what purpose? No new legal, social, or moral category is needed to cover these offenses. There is virtual unanimity that they are always and everywhere bad acts, and are consequently both tortious and criminal. Arguably the legal remedies available to attack such behavior are for one reason or other less than optimally effective. But the brouhaha about sexual harassment is not about crafting new remedies for old wrongs, but of recognizing new wrongs. At the other end of the spectrum, some of those most vociferous in raising the specter of sexual harassment use the label to cover acts that the rest of us view as relatively innocent, e.g., admiring the female physique or suggesting that men and women have fundamentally different interests and abilities.

Narrowing the definition

For the purpose of this discussion, a preliminary definition, that may be overly broad but represents an ordinary language interpretation of the words, will serve as a starting point. Sexual harassment is any unwelcome tactile, visual, or verbal communication of a sexual nature. As broad as this definition may appear it fails to cover some acts which have been labeled as sexual harassment, for example, the hiring of a strip-tease artist by a college fraternity. Three questions about sexual harassment need to be explored: (1) Is everything that falls within the definition evil and should it be condemned? (2) Is sexual harassment a class of behavior that is well suited to legal regulation? (3) Have recent legal assaults on this behavior been well aimed? The prevailing view implicitly answers each of these questions in the affirmative. Whether these answers are correct or not, for the sake of argument and because the conventional wisdom is still unexamined, the opposing perspective will be presented in the hope of generating more critical discourse.

Gender-specific tastes

Some claims of sexual harassment arise from the fact that men's tastes are different than women's. This is not to say that men and women do not differ among themselves, but certain kinds of behavior are more characteristically male and others more characteristically female. Men talk more often about sports while women discuss clothes; men read magazines like *Popular Mechanics* while women prefer *Good Housekeeping*. Such differences usually result in little more than men and women being bored or uneasy when forced into the company of a group of the opposite sex. Most of the sources of this discomfort could not reasonably be labeled as sexual harassment.

   Some types of behavior based on gender differences are of an erotic or quasi-erotic nature. Many men enjoy looking at pictures of naked women. Women seem to have less interest in looking at the naked bodies of either men or women. Men are more inclined to make sexual references in their speech and to tell off-color jokes, and more importantly to feel free doing this in a wider variety of social settings. Some women will find such discussions and language offensive and unpleasant, and here, because the discomfort is related to the erotic character of the activity, the sexual harassment label may apply.

Are there unwelcome sexual communications that do not rise to the level of a wrong? And do all communications that rise to that level simultaneously also rise to the level of tort? If so, then what lies in between will be a null set. Rather than discuss sexual harassment in the abstract, it will be more enlightening to examine the issue in light of concrete examples describing possibly unwelcome sexual communication. Two incidents, drawn from my family history, one involving my great-grandmother and the other myself, will serve as illustrations.

My great-grandfather was a renowned Orthodox rabbi in Lithuania and, after about 1925, in Philadelphia. Some time in the 1930s, his youngest daughter was betrothed to an Orthodox man. When my great-grandmother, a pious woman in her fifties, attempted to shake hands with her future son-in-law, he pulled away and objected that he would touch no woman other than his wife. Admittedly this man's behavior was extreme even by Orthodox standards, but his reaction was honest and reflected his religious beliefs. The prospect of touching a woman other than his wife, even in such an innocent and harmless manner, was offensive. To this man my great-grandmother's outstretched hand was a form of sexual harassment. From a very different portion of the social spectrum, I offer a personal experience. Shortly after I graduated from college I worked for a New York insurance company. One morning a young married woman employee with whom I had had no prior romantic relationship, literally pulled me into an office closet for a bit of sexual play. Some people in my position would have undoubtedly been outraged by the lady's behavior— I was not. I found her communication anything but unwelcome.

The definition of sexual harassment has become more, rather than less, elusive with use.

These incidents are not meant to be illustrative of all, most, or even many incidents of alleged sexual harassment. They differ most importantly from the core case in that the putative harasser in both cases was a woman and the victim was a man. Instead they are meant to show that the contours of appropriate behavior between the sexes, either as a prelude to, or part of, a sexual relationship, or simply as an aspect of ordinary social discourse, are not a fixed, universally known, or widely shared set of rules. And, to the extent that there are such rules there are a variety of views as to how they apply in different social environments. Even those who agree on where to draw the lines between the acceptable and the unacceptable will dispute whether violation of these rules should be treated as a faux pas, extremely gauche behavior, a tort, or a crime.

What social or legal rule makes sense in response to this cognitive, aesthetic, and ethical dispersion? A widely shared view of a liberal society has it that private acts between consenting adults are not the concern of society or the state. If a man's sexually aggressive behavior is accepted or approved of by the woman toward whom it is directed most of us would find no social and, *a fortiori*, no legal wrong. If a woman does not welcome a man's sexually aggressive behavior and he knows it and persists in it, he is guilty of at least a social wrong, and if his behavior is egregious enough, a legal one as well. Were this the whole world of possibilities, the social resolution, though perhaps not the legal one, would be easy enough. The first category would be permitted, the second would be condemned.

What if a man has made a mistake and misjudged the woman toward whom his communication is directed? For him the communication is an acceptable form of social intercourse that will perhaps be welcomed by the recipient, while to her it is not only unwelcome, but unacceptable. Should society treat these communications as a wrong? If the test of whether a communication is sexual harassment rests exclusively on the beliefs of the perpetrator, much that recipients find offensive will be permitted. On the other hand, if liability were to rest on the views of the recipient, much of what perpetrators do in all innocence would be condemned. Of course, we need choose neither of these endpoints as the legal or social rule. Nor need we choose the same legal and social rule, nor the same rule in all social contexts. But choose we must, and those choices are likely to force us to make some very difficult factual determinations.

Some of those most vociferous in raising the specter of sexual harassment use the label to cover acts that the rest of us view as relatively innocent.

To some the issue of sexual harassment may seem trivial. The tip of the iceberg that is revealed in court cases and newspaper articles is peripheral to most of our lives. But the iceberg that lies below the surface manifestations is immense. Unwelcome sexual advances by men, and the apprehension of such advances, are a real and unpleasant backdrop in the lives of women. Likewise, prosecutions, the fear of prosecutions, and more importantly, social disapproval and the fear of social disapproval for being too forward form the backdrop for men's lives. Acting out of their respective fears, members of both sexes adjust their behavior to the legal and social climate.

If there were no positive value to sexual communication, we could condemn any or all of it at much gain and little cost. But sexual communication is of enormous value. (Were it not for such communication, I would not be here to write this article, nor you to read it, for our parents would have never found a way to become our parents.) That men and women are at various times in their lives in the market for sexual partners is in general a good thing. Being in that market requires sexual communication.

Since sexual communication is such an important aspect of life, and takes place in the shadow of legal and social rules, even small changes in the rules can have a great impact on people's lives. If women and men are too fearful of contact with the opposite sex, the social preliminaries to romantic union may never occur. These are not idle or unfounded speculations. The market for romantic partners is a daunting one. We all know of men and women who, although they very much want to find a romantic partner, are counseled by their fears more than by their hopes, and so never make the leaps necessary to achieve their goal.

In traditional societies, and even in traditional corners of our own, there are well known, standard forms of courtship. Whether it is the use of a matchmaker or some other social device, people who grow up within a particular culture know the path they must tread. For most contemporary Americans these traditional forms are part of a charming ethnic heritage rather than a viable possibility.

In our open, dynamic, and multi-cultural society there is no one, or even a discrete, set of accepted ways in which men and women can make known their general availability, to say nothing of their attraction to a particular person. The dance of courtship is no longer a minuet, if it ever was. It is more like the variety of gyrations one might observe in a discotèque; there are no commonly shared steps. Acceptable sexual conduct covers the field from my great-aunt's husband to my co-worker of twenty-two years ago, and beyond. Sometimes we manage to signal sexual values through dress, occupation, location or activity, but often we do not. Prudes and prostitutes are forced to rub shoulders with one another, usually without visual signals of the values embodied in those shoulders. So, we continually confront the two-sided danger of either acting too aggressively, with all the attendant social and legal costs, or of acting too diffidently or not at all, and thereby losing an opportunity for a relationship. For those at the social extremes, the dance may be easiest; they know their steps. For those in the vast middle ground looking in both directions at the same time, the dance of courtship is more daunting. Learning the steps well enough to avoid stepping on, or tripping over, one's partner's feet is challenge enough. To do this under the threat of legal sanctions for overly aggressive but non-tortious behavior will drive men from the dance floor, and make it that much more difficult for men and women to find partners.

Standards of behavior and the law

The plea for recognition of, and sensitivity to, the delicate social institution we are affecting should not be interpreted as a call for no regulation of unwelcome sexual communication. Rather, it is a call for recognition of the benefits as well as the costs of aggressive sexual communication and for giving them proper weight in social and legal rules. It is seemingly natural to treat one's own standards of behavior as the appropriate legal and social norm. But a spirit of, if not complete, but at least of heightened legal, if not social, tolerance toward other people's communication is urgently needed. For some men, crude conversation is more natural and common—and not all women are put off by it. Different people have different tastes, and different social settings have different standards of accepted behavior. It is all too tempting to fall into a grand ethnocentrism in which the standards of our class, our generation, our religion, our social context, and our region are taken to be the standard of behavior for the whole society, and to seek to impose it on all through legislation.

Law is a vital tool of social regulation. Were it not for the very existence of law, and the reasonable set of property, contract, tort, and criminal rights and duties that it enforces, this nation would not be the rich, free, and generally pleasant place it is. Yet recognizing that law is on balance a fine thing does not mean that every aspect of life should be regulated by that institution.

Law, like all social institutions, has its strengths and weaknesses. Discussion of legal issues frequently takes place with the tacit assumption that law works costlessly, instantaneously, and with perfect accuracy. Were this assumption made explicit, no one would likely assent to it. But since the transaction costs of law are generally not explicitly modeled, discussion of legal reform is often carried on with the implicit assumption that costs are negligible and may be ignored. Thus for some commentators the question of whether to provide legal sanctions against a particular behavior collapses into determining whether that behavior is bad. The fact is that the law is a costly, inaccurate, and slow institution of social regulation and the remedies it offers are frequently unenforceable and not well tied to the wrong to be remedied. Even if it were possible theoretically to define a category of sexual harassment as evil, it may still not be sensible to impose legal sanctions on such behavior.

Sexual harassment in the workplace

Sexual harassment is an emerging legal category. Its current place in the legal architecture may be temporary or it may expand with time. Current federal prohibitions against sexual harassment derive from Section 703 of Title VII of the 1964 Civil Rights Act, which prohibits workplace discrimination based on sex. A series of cases, culminating with *Meritor Savings Bank v. Vinson*, found that certain forms of sexual harassment constituted prohibited sex discrimination.

There are three interesting questions about the legal standards that have thus far developed: (1) Are the appropriate parties being held liable? (2) Are the standards of liability sensible? (3) Is the workplace a particularly fruitful area to regulate?

Sexual harassment suits fall into two categories referred to in the legal literature as *quid pro quo* and "hostile environment." Under the first category the complainant asserts that because the sexual communication originates from the employee's supervisor, submission to unwelcome sexual communication is an express or implied condition of employment. The second category covers all other forms of unwelcome sexual communication in the workplace. The distinction between these two categories is important because it is tied to the most curious and suspect aspects of the law of sexual harassment, the designation of the employer as a defendant in the suit, and the standards of liability under which he will be judged. In virtually all sexual harassment cases the employer is made a party to the action and when liability is found, it is the employer who must foot the bill.

If women and men are too fearful of contact with the opposite sex, the social preliminaries to romantic union may never occur.

Because of its more liberal standards for establishing employer liability, *quid pro quo* cases are far more popular with plaintiffs than hostile environment cases. In a hostile environment case the complainant must show that the employer had notice of the hostile environment and failed to respond adequately. Notice is not identical with knowledge. If the employer knew or should have known of the harassment, that will be sufficient. In a *quid pro quo* case no such notice is required. The unwelcome sexual communication of a supervisor will be imputed to the employer. The employer cannot escape liability even if he had no way of knowing of the harassing behavior and had in place a strictly enforced policy against sexual harassment.

The employer's liability for an employee's sins is known as vicarious liability, which is a common feature of law. What makes it a peculiar, indeed a unique, application in the case of sexual harassment is that normally it is only employed when the acts of an employee are intended to serve the business interests of the employer. In the case of sexual harassment, the harassing behavior is not merely orthogonal to the employer's interest, but actually adverse to it. Let us assume that the employer is unaware of the harassment. The sexual harasser obviously attaches some positive value to the activity, and, equally obviously, his victims attach a negative value to it. Yet this is not merely a two-person game. Harassment costs that initially fall on the firm's female employees do not stop there. They will be passed on to the employer in the form of higher turnover rates, greater difficulty in filling positions at otherwise competitive wages, and a less productive working environment. The employer must ultimately pay the price of the harassment even if he is not legally liable.

What if the employer is aware of the harassment? Could he not and would he not at least reduce the harasser's income to reflect the psychic benefit the latter is receiving? While this is a theoretical possibility, the cost saving is unlikely to be sufficient to make up for the losses from the turnover of female employees. It is hard to imagine a situation in which the right to harass is financially more valuable to the harasser than the cost to the victim. Permitting male employees to use the workplace as a site to torment female employees with unwelcome sexual communication will always be a net cost to employers.

Aside from the unfairness of imposing liability on the employer for the harassment of one employee by another, a more important question is whether such liability conveys the appropriate incentives. Assuming that the behavior being prohibited is indeed something evil that should be legally prohibited and eliminated, this form of action is placing vicarious liability on the employer, who is the appropriate agent for optimally controlling this behavior.

At first blush vicarious liability seems an inefficient remedy in that it makes one of the wronged parties, rather than the wrongdoer, pay for the wrong to the other. It seems as though the employer must in effect pay twice for a wrong that was committed by the harasser, who pays nothing. This seemingly bizarre result will be partially mitigated by the employer's imposing some of the costs on the harassing employee, principally by dismissing him.

Even with this partial mitigation, the employer may be given too much incentive to deter harassment and may become overzealous. If the employer could costlessly and completely monitor all behavior in the workplace, and had a clear and precise definition of sexual harassment, he could prohibit all types of offensive behavior. But the world is not such a neat and clean place. Employers are generally not able to regulate the subtle and private behavior of their employees and, in this area, will be unsure of what to regulate. In the *Meritor* case, the Supreme Court, though willing to condemn sexual harassment, was loath to inform the world of the boundaries of this elusive cause of action. To the extent that employers fear sexual harassment suits, they will be inclined to draw the borders of acceptable male-female communication narrowly in order to distance their workplace environment from the invisible border of sexual harassment.

The workplace is an area where enforcement of laws against sexual harassment may yield great benefits. Time spent on the job takes up a good portion of most people's lives. Women invest a great deal of firm-specific human capital in their jobs and will incur substantial transaction costs if they must change jobs. Ensuring that women are not the subject of on-the-job sexual harassment will eliminate the possibility that they will be compelled to change jobs and suffer large losses because of sexual harassment. Before concluding that legal regulation is warranted, one must inquire into the marginal benefits of a legal remedy and of its potential costs. Although it is clear that eliminating sexual harassment in the workplace offers real gains, one wonders why the market has not already substantially eliminated it. Precisely because sexual harassment imposes costs on employers that will ultimately be shifted to the harasser, it is hard to see how true large-scale sexual harassment in the workplace can survive a market test.

In support of this proposition, the results of a sifting of the records of harassment cases indicate that a grossly disproportionate number of sexual harassment suits come from public sector employment. Since government employers do not face the market constraints of private employers and have less discretion in dismissing employees, they have less incentive and ability to discipline sexual harassment.

Even if it were possible theoretically to define a category of sexual harassment as evil, it may still not be sensible to impose legal sanctions on such behavior.

Still, even in a well functioning employment market some women are likely to be outraged by the sexual communications of fellow employees. Some of this will be sexual harassment, but perhaps some will not. The world of work is a congeries of different social settings. A woman can find employment everywhere from a Nevada whorehouse to a convent. From a sexual communication perspective is it reasonable to expect or to impose the same standards of behavior on each of these jobs and all those in between? Obviously not. While identifying one firm as a Brooklyn spice importer and another as a Manhattan real estate manager may not yield a clue as to the standards of sexual communication each expects and accepts from its employees, it is not unreasonable that they might differ on this continuum. In a free market both employers and employees can sort themselves on this social dimension as well as on all others. Some behavior that might otherwise appear as sexual harassment may be better viewed as a temporary mis-sorting of people in the employment market.

The greatest cost to regulating sexual harassment in the workplace is that for an increasing number of people the workplace represents by far the best avenue for finding and pursuing romantic interests. In our modern, open, dynamic society there are all too few social situations where men and women can meet and participate in the market for romantic partners without suffering this as the central purpose of the activity. At work they can flirt and in other ways get the ball rolling in a controlled, largely non-threatening environment. Should this marketplace be substantially damaged by regulations, the lives of those affected will be diminished. They will have more difficulty finding partners and will have to search in less attractive places.

This article reflects my scepticism about the social and legal category of sexual harassment and it may convey the sense that the law should bend over backwards to avoid entering this arena. This is not so. No argument is made for the abolition or curtailment of enforcement of traditional criminal and tort penalties for sexual offenses. On the contrary, they should be enforced more vigorously and be punished more harshly. Men being stronger and more aggressive than women, can—and some men will—take great advantage of them under the guise of ambiguous communication. We have a legal and social obligation to prevent or punish such behavior. But creating the undefined, politicized category of sexual harassment seems a poorly aimed and dangerous way to go about it.

Broad Definitions of Sexual Harassment Are Harmful

Wendy McElroy

Wendy McElroy is the editor of the university textbook Freedom, Feminism, and the State. *She is also a contributor to the* Freeman, *the monthly publication of the Foundation for Economic Education, Inc., in Irvington-on-Hudson, New York.*

Vague and overly broad definitions of sexual harassment currently used by government organizations, universities, and the court system not only victimize innocent men, they also harm the dignity of women. Allowing these institutions to mandate sexual attitudes is paternalistic toward women and threatens the liberty of adults of both sexes. The law should be used to protect against violence, not to coerce compliance with cultural attitudes and moral views. In cases of non-violent sexual harassment, women should stand up for themselves.

The issue of sexual harassment is shredding the fabric of the relations between men and women. Conservatives see laws against sexual harassment as further attacks on men and the free market. Feminists see sexual harassment as yet another outrage against women committed by men and the free market. Men fear to pay women compliments; some women feel harassed by every Southerner who calls them "honey." It is difficult to remember a time when there was less good will or humor between the sexes.

Meanwhile, employers rush to formulate policies they hope will insulate them from charges of sexual harassment, which the Equal Employment Opportunity Commission (EEOC) has ruled is a violation of Section 703 of Title VII of the 1964 Civil Rights Act. Because sexual harassment falls under Title VII (which defines the responsibilities of *employers*), it is employers who have become the targets of legal action. According to the EEOC guideline, employers are responsible for any sexual harassment within their businesses if they knew or should have known about the situation and if they took no immediate action to remedy the problem.

With all the controversy and liability that adheres to the issue of sexual harassment, one question becomes crucial: What is it?

Most feminists answer this question quickly. The National Organiza-

Wendy McElroy, "Sexual Harassment: What Is It?" *The Freeman,* June 1993. Courtesy of the Foundation for Economic Education.

tion for Women has offered this definition: "any repeated or unwarranted verbal or physical sexual advance, sexually explicit derogatory statement, or sexually discriminatory remark made by someone in the workplace, which is offensive or objectionable to the recipient, or which causes the recipient discomfort or humiliation, or which interferes with the recipient's job performance."

The legal system has evolved its own standards. In general, the judiciary has divided sexual harassment into two categories: (1) a *quid pro quo*, by which sexual favors are directly traded for professional gain; and (2) a hostile working environment, in which women are threatened. In 1980, the EEOC concurred with this guideline by finding that sexual harassment includes physical, verbal, and environmental abuse. This guideline was affirmed unanimously by the U.S. Supreme Court in 1986.

Men fear to pay women compliments; some women feel harassed by every Southerner who calls them "honey."

It is the more subtle form of sexual harassment—"a hostile working environment"—that has caused most of the controversy and confusion. Companies and institutions across the continent scramble to clarify the specifics of this litigious issue. The policy advanced by the Presidential Advisory Committee on Sexual Harassment at York University in Toronto, Canada, is fairly typical. York defined sexual harassment as: "unwanted sexual attention of a persistent or abusive nature, made by a person who knows or ought reasonably to know that such attention is unwanted; or, implied or expressed promise of reward for complying with a sexually oriented request; or, implied or expressed threat of reprisal, in the form of either actual reprisal or the denial of opportunity, for refusal to comply with a sexually oriented request; or, sexually oriented remarks and behavior which may reasonably be perceived to create a negative psychological and emotional environment for work and study."

Such policies clarify nothing. Words like "unwanted," "abusive," and "perceived" are too subjective to allow a real sense of what behavior constitutes sexual harassment. Further attempts to reach a definition seem only to muddy the issue. For example, in September 1989, Harvard University issued a guideline that removed any connection between behavior and intent. In other words, sexual harassment can occur even though the transgressor was a man of goodwill, with absolutely no intention of harm. In the section "Sexism in the Classroom," the Harvard guideline cautioned: "Alienating messages may be subtle and even unintentional, but they nevertheless tend to compromise the learning experience of both sexes. . . . For example, it is condescending to make a point of calling only upon women in a class on topics such as marriage and the family, imposing the assumption that only women have a natural interest in this area."

The 9th U.S. Circuit Court complicated the definition even more in a landmark decision. Judge Robert Beezer ruled that women are protected from any remark or behavior that a "reasonable woman" would have problems with. The court also embedded a double standard into the law by declaring that some behavior acceptable to men may be legally actionable by women.

No wonder men are resentful. They are being backed into a corner by accusations that seem to have no rules of evidence and little burden of proof.

Government is not part of the solution

I stumble into this quagmire with a unique perspective. As an individualist feminist, I believe not only in the rights of women, but also in their dignity. I also believe that the free market is the best way for women to protect both. In short, although I think sexual harassment is a real problem, I don't want government involved in the solution.

I do not include assault or threat of assault in this discussion of sexual harassment. Such behavior is clearly a legal matter. By "sexual harassment" I refer only to behavior that is non-violent, however offensive it may be. In this, the law should have no part.

Yet—because women resort to lawsuits—sexual harassment is almost always discussed in legal terms. What is the exact definition of the offense? What constitutes evidence?

I want to ask more fundamental questions: (1) Can the law effectively address this area? Is it even possible for the courts to adjudicate and punish attitudes toward women? (2) Should the law address this area? What is the cost and danger of doing so?

To answer the first question it is important to appreciate that sexual harassment is an expression of some men's attitudes toward women. Since I don't believe government can successfully mandate attitudes, I think legal remedies are doomed to failure—or worse. A change in attitude can come only from a change in the hearts and minds of people. This cannot be legislated.

To address the second question: Should government control the bad attitudes of its people? The very prospect of this is horrifying. The worst oppressor in the history of women has been the state. When the state claims to be "protecting" me through paternalistic policies, I tend to reach for my dignity, if not for my wallet.

But the main reason to avoid the legal system is not historical. It is simply that sexual harassment doesn't violate anyone's rights.

Although I think sexual harassment is a real problem, I don't want government involved in the solution.

What is the purpose of law in society? I believe the purpose of law is to protect individual rights, to protect self-ownership. Self-ownership means that every human being, simply by being human, has a moral and legal claim to his or her own body. Law comes into play only when a woman is a victim or initiator of force.

Contrast this with the view of law implicit in legislative attempts to prohibit or punish sexual harassment. Most feminists are trying to use the law to enforce a proper standard of morality or behavior, such as non-discrimination or respect for women. The law has become a means of enforcing "virtue." From this perspective, certain "bad" acts ought to be prohibited whether or not they are peaceful. In the case of sexual harassment, because men should not hold degrading opinions of women, the law punishes men whenever their unacceptable opinions are expressed in a public manner. The correct moral position becomes law.

I have great problems with imposing my moral views—however correct I believe them to be—on other people. I have trouble understanding how someone's bad attitude violates my rights. It seems to me that the most fundamental human freedom is the right to weigh evidence and reach a conclusion. People have a right to reach conclusions that I find wrong and offensive: They have a right to consider me inferior because of my sex. If I can take someone to court over his or her attitude toward me, this says that I have a right to tell them what opinions they are legally allowed to hold. More than this—it says that the government has a right to regulate opinions.

In *Time* magazine, Ellen Frankel Paul of Bowling Green State University commented on this grim prospect: "Do we really want legislators and judges delving into our most intimate private lives? Deciding when a look is a leer and when a leer is a civil rights offense? Should people have a legally enforceable right not to be offended by others? At some point, the price for such protection is the loss of both liberty and privacy rights."

Which standard?

Any attempt to impose "thought control" would be the death of individual freedom. And this is a freedom to which the weakest members of society (such as women) should cling. If moral and cultural standards can be imposed by law, ultimately it will not be the weak who decide "which standard."

Moreover, if government has the right to control and punish cultural attitudes, where will the cut-off point be? If it is proper to punish bad sexual attitudes, why not bad religious ones? Yet the political control of bad attitudes is precisely what sexual harassment laws are about.

A driving force behind these laws is socialist or radical feminism. In turn, this form of feminism is a building block of political correctness—the movement that considers virtually all of Western culture to be racist and sexist. Those who are politically correct seek to correct this injustice by championing the victims of Western civilization.

Dinesh D'Souza, in his controversial book *Illiberal Education*, defined these "victims": "Those who suffer from the effects of Western colonialism in the third world, as well as race and gender discrimination in America." In other words, women and minorities.

Sexual harassment is an expression of some men's attitudes toward women.

For the good of society, a persecution of "wrong" attitudes toward women has begun. I believe that a new inquisition is under way, one that is being driven by the political correctness movement. It is—in large part—an economic inquisition. One of the main battlefields has become the workplace. The heretics to be punished are those businessmen who do not express the politically correct attitude toward women.

And yet in condemning the political exploitation of abused women, I do not want to deny the importance of sexual harassment as a problem. Sexual harassment is an offense to the dignity and decency of human beings. To forswear the legal system is not to abandon the right of protest.

Many well intentioned men are like those who have never suffered from racism; they have a natural tendency to dismiss the suffering as not real. Many women share this reaction. Even the insightful commentator Jane S. Shaw declared:

> I'm skeptical about sexual harassment simply because during more than twenty years in the workforce, I never experienced anything that I would call sexual harassment. I have, however, experienced some awkward on-the-job situations that were related to sex. . . . They undoubtedly reflected uncertainty about appropriate behavior, especially as mores changed over the past couple of decades.

I cannot comment on Ms. Shaw's personal perceptions or her experiences. But I can add my own. For the last few years, I have achieved a modest status as a writer of documentaries. During this period, I have experienced no sexual harassment whatsoever.

Before this, I worked at whatever job I could in order to pursue writing at night. I entered the workforce at the lowest rung. In other words, I was an interchangeable unit. When I was a secretary, thousands of other women could have performed my job as well as I did. When I was an interchangeable unit, I relied heavily upon the common decency of my employers, who were men. Most were benevolent; a few lived up to the worst stereotypes of predatory men; one crossed the line into assault. Although I do not forgive any of the humiliations, only the assault was a matter for the law.

Most men are decent people who are busy living their lives. When the shrill and accusing cry of aggrieved women reaches their ears, they have the natural impulse to turn away. Because they see nothing of themselves in the male caricatures being presented, they dismiss the women as hysterical or man-hating. On at least one level, I can't blame them. Much of men's reactions come from the fact that women are using force, in the form of law, to impose standards of behavior upon them. And force is the death of discussion or sympathy.

Sexual harassment doesn't violate anyone's rights.

Men are becoming so angry about sexual harassment that they are losing their sense of compassion for abused women. Every word in the workplace might become evidence in a legal proceeding. To them, women's cry for decent treatment resembles a witch hunt. Men's compassion has been replaced by exasperated demands for a list of things they are no longer allowed to say or do, for a clear definition of what constitutes sexual harassment. This is a fair question.

I freely admit that I cannot clearly define sexual harassment any more than I can clearly define what is offensive. Sexual harassment is a subjective term that depends on the personalities and cultural backgrounds of the people involved.

But to say that the edges of a problem are gray, rather than hard and clean, is not to say that it does not exist. Racism is difficult to define, yet few people would deny its existence. Subjectivity is a good reason for keeping both sexual harassment and racism out of the court system, where the law requires a clear point of enforcement. But it is not a reason to ignore the pain of abused women.

The free market is not an arena of justice: It was never meant to be. It is simply a coordinating mechanism, by which supply and demand are balanced. Equally, the court system does not protect my dignity: That is not its proper purpose. It exists to protect my rights. It is up to me to stand up and protest any assault on dignity. Those who tell me to be silent or walk away are denying that I have this right of protest. No wonder so many women are turning to the law.

I would like to believe that my commitment to individual rights and to women's dignity are not in conflict. I do believe that an attack on sexism is not an attack on the free market: It does not deny the right of businessmen to hire and fire according to their own personal judgment. It does say: If an employer has the legal right to fire me, I have the legal right to protest, publicly and loudly, not from the witness stand of a courtroom, but from whatever platforms a free society allows.

Those who are hostile to the free market are using the issue of sexual harassment to gain political control of the workplace. They are having an easy time of it, because they seem to be the only ones addressing a genuine problem. The very intensity of women's indignation over sexual harassment should have alerted people to the need for a solution. But by blaming women, businesses have dismissed the problem. They have left it to others to voice the growing wellspring of anger.

9

Broad Definitions of Sexual Harassment May Be Counterproductive for Businesses

J.H. Foegen

J.H. Foegen is a professor of business at Winona State University in Minnesota.

Businesses may find that the all-inclusive definitions of sexual harassment currently in use will harm their workplace environment. Since men and women appear to interpret sexual harassment differently, and since most of those accused of harassment are men, in a corporate setting men may choose to ignore their female coworkers rather than risk being charged with sexual harassment. This separation would be damaging both for the employees, whose work would suffer in such an environment, and for the productivity of the company.

Biology prevents men and women from ignoring one another—in the workplace as elsewhere. Heightened sensitivity regarding sexual harassment has resulted from the Clarence Thomas confirmation hearings in 1991. Despite the admitted positive aspects, new awareness risks a productivity-reducing chill in the workplace climate. Most American companies can ill afford this as they compete internationally and pursue total quality management.

After controversial hearings concerning allegations of sexual harassment, the United States Senate confirmed Judge Clarence Thomas to the Supreme Court. The vote was fifty-two to forty-eight. Workplace fallout from those hearings will undoubtedly continue for a long time, as employers, supervisors, and workers of both genders try to accommodate greater sensitivity to an old problem made newly urgent. A potential danger is that either deliberately, or as an unconscious, knee-jerk reaction, males will in self-defense tend to ignore women coworkers. Wary of even possible charges of harassment, they will try to play it safe.

J.H. Foegen, "The Double Jeopardy of Sexual Harassment," *Business and Society Review*, Summer 1992. Reprinted with permission.

Much of the problem hinges upon definition; existing laws are help-ful but hardly satisfactory. Though improving gradually, the laws remain less than helpful in specific situations. Equal Employment Opportunity Commission (EEOC) guidelines, which have been updated several times since 1980, flag two basic kinds of sexual impropriety. The blatant, now relatively uncontroversial kind involves a quid pro quo: sleep with me or else. The more subtle type, still arguable in its near-infinite ramifications, concerns "hostile environment." Offensive behavior not yet addressed satisfactorily under the law includes jokes, leers, displays of girlie calen-dars, and refusing to take "no" for an answer in dating.

In typical legalese, the EEOC defined sexual harassment as: "unwel-come sexual advances, requests for sexual favors, and other verbal or physical contact or communication of a sexual nature when submission to such conduct is made either explicitly or implicitly a term or condition of an individual's employment; submission to or rejection of such con-duct by an individual is used as a basis for employment decisions affect-ing such individual; or such conduct has the purpose or effect of unrea-sonably interfering with an individual's work performance, or creating an intimidating, hostile, or offensive work environment." Bringing such lan-guage down to earth, one of the nation's major labor unions, the United Auto Workers, spells things out more clearly in a brochure available from its women's department.

Heightened sensitivity regarding sexual harassment has resulted from the Clarence Thomas confirmation hearings.

Noting that harassment violates Title VII of the Civil Rights Act, the union stresses that represented employees are also protected by the union's constitution, and often by negotiated contract language. All this is meaningless, however, unless the individual takes a stand, and says "no." The UAW also notes that, while most of this undesirable contact is aimed at women, its policies also cover incidents in which men are vic-tims, either of women or of other men.

Examples of nonverbal harassment are also cited. They include cer-tain looks, gestures, leering, ogling, pictures, and cartoons. Physical of-fensiveness includes touching, pinching, rubbing, or "accidentally" brushing breasts or buttocks. The union advises members that, in addi-tion to saying no, they should tell the offender they do not like what is going on. They should also document times, dates, and locations where harassment occurs, what was said or done to them, and their responses. Looking for other victims, sometimes people who were fired or who quit suddenly, is also advised, as is supporting others facing the problem.

Perhaps even more practical is the commonsense approach taken by Corning, the well-known kitchenware manufacturer. The company rec-ommends that employees consider four questions, according to *The Econ-omist:* Would you do it before your spouse or parents? Would you do it in front of a same-sex colleague? Would you like it reported in the local newspaper? Does it need saying or doing at all?

The courts, meanwhile, have tried to refine their concept of what is allowable. The test first evolved from a "reasonable man" standard to a more restrictive "reasonable person" one. And in 1991 a federal court in Florida ruled that the standard was what would be offensive in the perception of a reasonable woman.

Earlier, in the 1986 case *Meritor Savings Bank v. Vinson*, the Supreme Court flagged possible employer liability if a policy on sexual harassment was absent. Many agree, however, that formal statements are not enough; preventative action is needed. Training sessions for both sexes are highly desirable, recognizing that too many people still do not realize that once-common practices are no longer acceptable.

Perceptions between the sexes

The change impacting both genders today seems to hinge upon different perceptions between the sexes. During and after the Thomas confirmation hearings, countless stories were reported in the press. One consultant told *Business Week*, for example, that "when men look at sexual harassment, they tend to think of touching. Women tend to consider the hostile work environment—her chest being stared at, the sexual jokes." And syndicated columnist Ellen Goodman quoted a political scientist and law professor from the University of Michigan, who sees a related contrast: "Men see the sex first and miss the coercion. Women see the coercion and miss the sex." Regardless of seemingly intractable differences, the professor is not fatalistic about change. He says our justice system is convinced that empathy is possible. People can "get in another's head," given a willingness to do so.

Ignoring one another completely in the workplace, regardless of motivation, is of course unlikely, if not impossible. Such an extreme, however, is far from necessary. Even a degree of wariness can hinder productivity; people sense intuitively when interpersonal tension exists. Ample evidence can be found that such wariness is present already, with the end of the harassment controversy nowhere in sight.

Bewilderment about what is permissible continues to be reported—and what appears in print is undoubtedly only the tip of the iceberg. One manager, for example, told *Business Week* about a female colleague putting her hand lightly on a man's shoulder. Another woman rushed up and said excitedly, "Oh, no, don't do that!" Another woman at a large insurance company told the magazine, "In my office now, if we say something that could be misconstrued as sexist, the guys pop up and say, 'That's sexual harassment.'"

Even a degree of wariness can hinder productivity; people sense intuitively when interpersonal tension exists.

While the Hill-Thomas controversy was at its height, a *Washington Post* editor pointedly asked, "Can we women and men of the work force never again laugh together at the latest off-color joke? Can we not exchange compliments or (discreetly) discuss the physical attributes of passersby in the office halls?" Similarly, as Ellen Goodman reported, one boss greeted his secretary, "Good morning—or is that sexual harassment?" More likely than not, he was only half kidding; the question can be seen as symbolic of a chilled atmosphere.

Perhaps most representative was the observation of an employee of the Union Pacific Railroad shortly after the Thomas hearings. "I have already noticed the difference at work. As a matter of fact, I asked a couple of ladies—they had even noticed the difference. Men are not speaking to them as . . . in the past," he told the Associated Press. He said he thought coworkers of both sexes were made nervous by the harassment issue.

Sex-saturated society

Behind the short-run feelings of unease created by greater awareness are at least two broad-scale problems that together offer a meaningful framework. The climate in which workplace harassment occurs is itself an issue. One editorial, which appeared in *The National Catholic Register*, was right on target: "Society cannot have it both ways. It cannot encourage and subsidize sleaze in art, film, literature, advertising, and television—and then expect to have work atmospheres that are free of sexual harassment. Our entire culture is so saturated and obsessed with sexual imagery that no one should be surprised when that obsession is expressed in the workplace." Individuals can, of course, control their actions; even in a sex-saturated society they do not have to harass coworkers. Still, a valid point is made.

Another wide-ranging aspect of the harassment issue concerns communication generally. Whatever deficiencies exist in an organization are magnified when an emotional issue like sexual behavior surfaces. Intentions are often misinterpreted; it is often hard to tell whether comments are innocent, intended to demean, or somewhere between. Unfortunately, this can also provide a handy rationalization for any who intend to harass. On the other hand, having to watch every word said can be irritating too, especially when no offense is meant. It seems as though the presumption of innocence until proved guilty has been turned on its head. It can be disconcerting.

Being on guard constantly against giving offense sexually inhibits all other communication too. You can never tell when someone might take something the wrong way. The situation can even deteriorate into another us-versus-them confrontation, much like that which exists between some labor unions and management. When total quality management is being stressed widely, such an atmosphere is counterproductive. Output, teamwork, competitiveness, and a pleasant work environment all suffer.

Without denying the problem's seriousness, it is instructive that confusion and wariness can fuse in a superficially humorous way. In one poll, for example, one in seven men responded that they would be offended if they were the object of sexual advances in the workplace; three-quarters of the polled women said so. But three-quarters of the men said they would be flattered.

This discussion should not be interpreted as defending sexual harassment by anyone at any time. The whole situation should, in fact, be a nonissue. For whatever perverse reasons, however, it remains one. Perhaps the bottom line must rest ultimately upon goodwill, once sufficient understanding has been achieved. While biology cannot be ignored, it controls intelligent employees of integrity only in a primitive sense. Those who, in fairness and good conscience, conduct themselves properly, can set the pace by being good examples. Any initial chill can disappear or remain negligible, given goodwill all around.

10

Current Sexual Harassment Definitions Are Inappropriate for Schools

Mona Charen

Mona Charen is a nationally syndicated columnist.

New studies have concluded that sexual harassment is a serious problem in primary and secondary schools. However, applying today's definitions of sexual harassment to the schools is inappropriate. The sexually uncouth behavior of today's children does not constitute sexual harassment; rather, it reflects the vulgar, violent, and sexually explicit nature of America's media and culture.

I'm glad, I suppose, that sexual harassment is being condemned in the national press. The most recent example is a study commissioned by the American Association of University Women showing that the behavior is widespread among junior high and high school students nationwide.

But there is a distressing lack of clarity in the discussion of the issue, and I fear that a facile and superficial understanding of the problem will lead to simplistic and formulaic solutions—like consciousness-raising classes—that will skirt the true problem.

In the first place, any study that purports to find that 81 percent of students are victims of something (other than math quizzes) is suffering from overbroad definitionitis. So it is with this study conducted by Louis Harris and Associates. According to the study's usage, sexual harassment includes everything from having clothing torn off and being forced to perform sexual acts, to unwanted sexual jokes, gestures or looks. It is hardly surprising that by the latter loose standard, more than four-fifths of the students defined themselves as victims of sexual harassment.

Still, the fact that more than 60 percent of girls and 40 percent of boys aged 13 to 17 report that they have been "touched, grabbed or pinched in a sexual way" is evidence of something. But what?

That's the critical question. What is going on here? Is this the early blooming of the kind of sexual harassment that the feminists claim is a male-invented weapon to subjugate and humiliate women? Is that what

Mona Charen, "Sexual Harassment Is Just Vulgar Behavior," *Conservative Chronicle*, June 16, 1993. Reprinted by permission of Mona Charen and Creators Syndicate.

73

11- and 12-year-old boys are thinking?

I submit that we are not dealing here with a political problem of the war between the sexes. We are dealing with a cultural problem. The overwhelming vulgarity and seaminess that has come to dominate our culture in entertainment, mores and manners has borne predictable fruit. We are raising children and adolescents who think nothing of telling an 11-year-old girl on a school bus to have oral sex with her father (an actual case), or threatening a 12-year-old with rape.

The overwhelming vulgarity and seaminess that has come to dominate our culture in entertainment, mores and manners has borne predictable fruit.

Is this shocking? Only to the inattentive. Turn on network television any night of the week, and you will get an earful of coarse language, puerile double entendres and vulgar innuendoes. And that's during the family hour. Many of the magazines sold at supermarket checkout counters look like soft porn. Even video games (aimed exclusively at children) are so sexually violent that one manufacturer has agreed to start labeling the programs to enable parents to monitor what kids are seeing. The language, violence and sexual content of movies is so raw that many adults would hesitate to attend with their aging parents—though they might look the other way when their 14-year-old son sees them again and again.

Junior high vulgarity

How can parents, who allow their pre-pubescent daughters to wear bras on the outside of their clothing, like Madonna, the teen idol, be surprised to learn that coarse sexual talk and manners are common in the halls of junior high schools?

This culture, awash in cheap sexual thrills, has lost sight of the noble, the fine and the uplifting. Sex is too important to be cheapened without disastrous results. When we demean sex, we demean our humanity.

My religion, Judaism, is a religion of laws. There are thousands of laws regulating every aspect of human conduct. But there are more rules about sex and eating than anything else. Why? Because those are behaviors we share with animals—and it is doubly important that we invest them with meaning, order and sanctity.

If our kids are behaving like boors, grabbing at one anothers' bodies, leaving obscene notes in lockers and spreading sexual rumors, as the study indicates, it is because we adults have permitted them to be instructed by 2 Live Crew, *Married with Children* and *The Love Connection*. It is because we have long since abandoned modesty, respect and chastity as relics of an irrelevant past. It is poignant that the new freedom has left the children so unhappy.

What is called "sexual harassment" is really just vulgar behavior, and it can be added to the list of accomplishments of the sexual revolution—right under epidemic of teen-age pregnancy, and just above AIDS.

11

Current Definitions of Sexual Harassment Should Not Apply to Academia

Katie Roiphe

Feminist Katie Roiphe is the author of The Morning After: Sex, Fear, and Feminism on Campus. *She is pursuing a Ph.D. in English at Princeton University.*

On college campuses around the country, sexual harassment, like acquaintance rape, has become a serious issue for women's groups. Doctrinaire feminist groups on campuses have taken current definitions of sexual harassment and applied them to every situation they find "uncomfortable." The result is virtual sexual harassment hysteria vilifying male professors and students alike. This hysterical atmosphere inhibits free speech and undermines the education environment.

For generations, women have talked and written and theorized about their problems with men. But theories about patriarchy tumble from abstraction when you wake up next to it in the morning. Denouncing male oppression clashes with wanting him anyhow. From playgrounds to consciousness-raising groups, from suffragette marches to prochoice marches, women have been talking their way through this contradiction for a long time.

Sometimes my younger sister and I go out for coffee and talk about our relationships. We analyze everything: why he acts that way, how unfair this is, how we shouldn't be waiting for his call, and how we have better things to do with our time anyway. How men are always like that, and we are always like this, and our conversation goes on, endless, pleasurable, interesting, over many refills, until we go home and wait for their calls.

"The man question"

Heterosexual desire inevitably raises conflicts for the passionate feminist, and it's not an issue easily evaded. Sooner or later feminism has to address "the man question." But this is more than just a practical question of pro-

From *The Morning After: Sex, Fear, and Feminism on Campus* by Katie Roiphe. Copyright ©1993 by Katherine Ann Roiphe. Reprinted by permission of Little, Brown and Company.

creation, more than the well-worn translation of personal into political. It's also a question for the abstract, the ideological, the furthest reaches of the feminist imagination.

Charlotte Perkins Gilman, a prominent feminist writing at the turn of the [20th] century, found a fictional solution to the conflict between sex and feminism in her utopian novel, *Herland*. Her solution is simple: there is no sexual desire. Even after the male anthropologists arrive with their worldly lusts, the women of Herland remain unruffled. Everything runs smoothly and rationally in Herland, and through the entire course of the book none of the women harbors any sexual feelings, toward men or toward each other. They magically reproduce by parthenogenesis, and motherhood is their driving passion.

Gilman erases whatever problems arise from sexual involvements with men in her happy, if sterile, vision of clean streets, clean hearts, clean minds. In her sociological work, *Women and Economics*, Gilman applies the same device—obliterating the source of conflict—to another site of struggle. She conceives of houses without kitchens as the solution to women's household drudgery. The problem is that most people want kitchens, and most people want sex.

The word "uncomfortable" echoes through all the literature on sexual harassment.

Many of today's feminists, in their focus on sexual harassment, share Gilman's sexual politics. In their videos, literature, and workshops, these feminists are creating their own utopian visions of human sexuality. They imagine a world where all expressions of sexual appreciation are appreciated. They imagine a totally symmetrical universe, where people aren't silly, rude, awkward, excessive, or confused. And if they are, they are violating the rules and are subject to disciplinary proceedings.

A Princeton pamphlet declares that "sexual harassment is unwanted sexual attention that makes a person feel uncomfortable or causes problems in school or at work, or in social settings."[1] The word "uncomfortable" echoes through all the literature on sexual harassment. The feminists concerned with this issue, then, propose the right to be comfortable as a feminist principle.

The difficulty with these rules is that, although it may infringe on the right to comfort, unwanted sexual attention is part of nature. To find wanted sexual attention, you have to give and receive a certain amount of unwanted sexual attention. Clearly, the truth is that if no one was ever allowed to risk offering unsolicited sexual attention, we would all be solitary creatures.

The category of sexual harassment, according to current campus definitions, is not confined to relationships involving power inequity. Echoing many other common definitions of sexual harassment, Princeton's pamphlet warns that "sexual harassment can occur between two people regardless of whether or not one has power over the other."[2] The weight of this definition of sexual harassment, then, falls on gender instead of status.[3]

In current definitions of sexual harassment, there is an implication that gender is so important that it eclipses all other forms of power. The driving idea behind these rules is that gender itself is a sufficient source of power to constitute sexual harassment. Catharine MacKinnon, an early theorist of sexual harassment, writes that "situations of co-equal power—among co-workers or students or teachers—are difficult to see as examples of sexual harassment unless you have a notion of male power. I think we lie to women when we call it not power when a woman is come on to by a man who is not her employer, not her teacher."[4] With this description, MacKinnon extends the province of male power beyond that of tangible social power. She proposes using the words "sexual harassment" as a way to name what she sees as a fundamental social and political inequity between men and women. Following in this line of thought, Elizabeth Grauerholz, a sociology professor, conducted a study about instances of male students harassing their female professors, a phenomenon she calls "contrapower harassment."[5]

Recently, at the University of Michigan, a female teaching assistant almost brought a male student up on charges of sexual harassment. She was offended by an example he used in a paper about polls—a few sentences about "Dave Stud" entertaining ladies in his apartment when he receives a call from a pollster—and she showed the paper to the professor of the class. He apparently encouraged her to see the offending example as an instance of sexual harassment. She decided not to press charges, although she warned the student that the next time anything else like this happened, in writing or in person, she would not hesitate. The student wisely dropped the course. To understand how this student's paragraph about Dave Stud might sexually harass his teacher, when he has much more to lose than she does, one must recognize the deeply sexist assumptions about male-female relations behind the teaching assistant's charge.

The idea that a male student can sexually harass a female professor, overturning social and institutional hierarchy, solely on the basis of some primal or socially conditioned male power over women is insulting. The mere fact of being a man doesn't give the male student so much power that he can plow through social hierarchies, grabbing what he wants, intimidating all the cowering female faculty in his path. The assumption that female students or faculty must be protected from the sexual harassment of male peers or inferiors promotes the regrettable idea that men are natively more powerful than women.

Men and power

Even if you argue, as many do, that *in this society* men are simply much more powerful than women, this is still a dangerous train of thought. It carries us someplace we don't want to be. Rules and laws based on the premise that all women need protection from all men, because they are so much weaker, serve only to reinforce the image of women as powerless.

Our female professors and high-ranking executives, our congresswomen and editors, are every bit as strong as their male counterparts. They have earned their position of authority. To declare that their authority is vulnerable to a dirty joke from someone of inferior status just because that person happens to be a man is to undermine their position. Female authority is not (and should not be seen as) so fragile that it shatters at the first sign of male sexuality. Any rules saying otherwise strip women, in the public eye, of their hard-earned authority.

Since common definitions of sexual harassment include harassment between peers, the emphasis is not on external power structures, but on inner landscapes. The boundaries are subjective, the maps subject to mood. According to the Equal Employment Opportunity Commission's definition, any conduct may be deemed sexual harassment if it "has the purpose or effect of unreasonably interfering with an individual's work or academic performance or creating an intimidating, hostile or offensive working or academic environment." The hostility or offensiveness of a working environment is naturally hard to measure by objective standards. Such vague categorization opens the issue up to the individual psyche.

The clarity of the definition of sexual harassment as a "hostile work environment" depends on a universal code of conduct, a shared idea of acceptable behavior that we just don't have. Something that makes one person feel uncomfortable may make another person feel great. At Princeton, counselors reportedly tell students, If you feel sexually harassed then chances are you were. At the university's Terrace Club, the refuge of fashionable, left-leaning, black-clad undergraduates, there is a sign supporting this view. It is downstairs, on a post next to the counter where the beer is served, often partially obscured by students talking, cigarettes in hand: "What constitutes sexual harassment or intimidating, hostile or offensive environment is to be defined by the person harassed and his/her own feelings of being threatened or compromised." This relatively common definition of sexual harassment crosses the line between being supportive and obliterating the idea of external reality.

The categories become especially complicated and slippery when sexual harassment enters the realm of the subconscious. The Princeton guide explains that "sexual harassment may result from a conscious or unconscious action, and can be subtle or blatant." Once we move into the area of the subtle and unconscious, we are no longer talking about a professor systematically exploiting power for sex. We are no longer talking about Hey, baby, sleep with me or I'll fail you. To hold people responsible for their subtle, unconscious actions is to legislate thought, an ominous, not to mention difficult, prospect.

The idea of sexual harassment—and clearly when you are talking about the subtle and unconscious, you are talking about an idea—provides a blank canvas on which students can express all of the insecurities, fears, and confusions about the relative sexual freedom of the college experience. Sexual harassment is everywhere: it crops up in dinner conversations and advertisements on television, all over women's magazines and editorial pages. No one can claim that Anita Hill is an unsung heroine. It makes sense that teenagers get caught up in the Anita Hill fury; they are particularly susceptible to feeling uncomfortable about sexuality, and sexual harassment offers an ideology that explains "uncomfortable" in political terms. The idea of sexual harassment displaces adolescent uneasiness onto the environment, onto professors, onto older men.

Open doors create barriers

The heightened awareness of the potential for sexual encroachment creates an atmosphere of suspicion and distrust between faculty and students. Many professors follow an unwritten rule: never close the door to your office when you and a female student are inside. One professor told a male teaching assistant I know that closing the door to his office with a student inside is an invitation to charges of sexual harassment. If keeping the door open is not enough to ward off the perception or reality of sexual harassment, the authors of *The Lecherous Professor*, an early book of essays about sexual harassment, warn faculty that "if a situation is potentially threatening, a colleague can always be asked to sit in on student-teacher conferences."[6] Although these policies may reduce the likelihood of sexual harassment charges, they also increase the amount of sexual tension between students and professors. The open door or the extra faculty member only draws attention to the potential for a sexual dynamic between professor and student. They promote the idea that professors are more interested in bodies than minds.

The inflamed rhetoric against harassment implies that all women are potential victims and all men are potential harassers. "Men in the Academy," an essay in the book *Ivory Power*, vilifies the male academic so effectively that the author is forced to acknowledge that "nonetheless, not all male professors harass female students."[7] That this need even be said is evidence that this perspective is spiraling out of control.

The irony is that these open doors, and all that they symbolize, threaten to create barriers between faculty and students. In the present hypersensitive environment, caution and better judgment can lead professors to keep female students at a distance. It may be easier not to pursue friendships with female students than to risk charges of sexual harassment and misunderstood intentions. The rhetoric surrounding sexual harassment encourages a return to formal relations between faculty and students.

> *To find wanted sexual attention, you have to give and receive a certain amount of unwanted sexual attention.*

The university, with its emphasis on intellectual exchange, on the passionate pursuit of knowledge, with its strange hours and unworldly citizens, is theoretically an ideal space for close friendships. The flexible hours combined with the intensity of the academic world would appear to be fertile ground for connections, arguments over coffee. Recently, reading a biography of the poet John Berryman, who was also a professor at Princeton in the forties, I was struck by stories about his students crowding into his house late into the night to talk about poetry. These days, an informal invitation to a professor's house till all hours would be a breach of propriety. As the authors of *The Lecherous Professor* warn, "Contacts outside of class deserve thought. Student-teacher conferences should be held in appropriate settings."[8]

In combating sexual harassment, feminists must necessarily distrust the intimacy of the academic environment. They must necessarily distrust a male professor having lunch with a female student. In *Ivory Power*, this is offered as a male professor's typical attitude: "In a classroom setting it is entirely appropriate that personal and professional lives be separated. However[,] undergraduates doing [honors] research and graduate students [are] becoming junior colleagues; a close personal relationship is to be encouraged."[9] In the eyes of the author, this is an outrageous position, one that precipitates sexual harassment. That this professor's harmless comment is so seditious, that it is used as an illustration of dangerous attitudes among male faculty members, indicates the vehemence of the feminist desire for separation between professors and students.

Feminists concerned with sexual harassment must fight for an immutable hierarchy, for interactions so cleansed of personal interest there can be no possibility of borders crossed. Although this approach to education may reduce the number of harmful connections between teachers and students, it may also reduce the number of meaningful connections. The problem with the chasm solution to faculty-student relations is that for graduate students, and even for undergraduates, connections with professors are intellectually as well as professionally important.

In an early survey of sexual harassment, a law student at Berkeley wrote that in response to fears of sexual harassment charges, "the male law school teachers ignore female students . . . this means that we are afforded [fewer] academic opportunities than male students."[10] Many male professors have confirmed that they feel more uncomfortable with female students than with male students, because of all the attention given to sexual harassment. They may not "ignore" their female students, but they keep them at arm's length. They feel freer to forge friendships with male students.

The overstringent attention given to sexual harassment on campuses breeds suspicion; it creates an environment where imaginations run wild, charges can seem to materialize out of thin air, and both faculty and students worry about a friendly lunch. The repercussions for the academic community, let alone the confused freshman, can be many and serious.

The rights of professors

In an excessive effort to purge the university of sexual corruption, many institutions have violated the rights of the professors involved by neglecting to follow standard procedures. Since sexual harassment is a relatively recent priority, "standard procedures" are themselves new, shrouded, and shaky. Charges of sexual harassment are uncharted territory, and fairness is not necessarily the compass.

In a recent case a tenured professor at a prominent university was dismissed in a unilateral administrative action, without a faculty hearing, legal counsel, or the calling of witnesses in his defense. Some professors have been suspended indefinitely without a sense of when or what would end the suspension. As an official of the American Association of College Professors framed the problem, "There tends to be publicizing of names at too early a stage, and trigger-quick action to suspend without suggestion of immediate harm."[11]

The American Association of College Professors has issued a statement about such overzealous enforcement of sexual harassment policy, explaining that "sexual harassment—which committee A certainly does not condone—is not somehow so different from other kinds of sanctionable misconduct as to permit the institution to render judgement and to penalize without having afforded due process."[12] This statement emphasizes the danger in looking at sexual harassment as an issue somehow more pressing, more serious, more important, than other disciplinary problems. The reason due process is thrown to the wind is that the pressure is so great, and the issue regarded as so delicate and mysterious, that administrations are overcompensating. They feel that if they deal with the issue swiftly, they are being responsive.

In *The Lecherous Professor*, authors Billie Wright Dziech and Linda Weiner explain why feminists are not concerned with due process:

> Let a single 110-pound nineteen-year-old muster the courage to

complain about being fondled or threatened by a Shakespeare professor, and Latin professors, geographers, physicists, architects, engineers, and lawyers are likely to rediscover the bonds that unite them. They will as a chorus mouth platitudes about loyalty to the institution, academic freedom and due process. They will suddenly remember the lyrics to the alma mater.[13]

For Dziech and Weiner, academic freedom and due process are simply more platitudes generated by the old-boy network. They dismiss any concern about fairness with their image of the ranks of male professionals united against the slim victim. Sexual harassment has assumed such grand proportions in the minds of these feminists that they are not concerned with the machinations of the disciplinary system, however Kafkaesque. To many feminists, like Dziech and Weiner, who are interested in cleansing the university of harassers, a few casualties of justice along the way seem like a small price to pay.

The university has become so saturated with the idea of sexual harassment that it has begun to affect minute levels of communication. Like "date rape," the phrase "sexual harassment" is frequently used, and it does not apply only to extremes of human behavior. Suddenly everyday experience is filtered through the strict lens of a new sexual politics. Under fierce political scrutiny, behavior that once seemed neutral or natural enough now takes on ominous meanings. You may not even realize that you are a survivor of sexual harassment.

A student tells me that she first experienced sexual harassment when she came to college. She was at a crowded party, leaning against a wall, and a big jock came up to her, placed his hands at either side of her head, and pretended to lean against her, saying, So, baby, when are we going out? All right, he didn't touch me, she says, but he invaded my space. He had no right to do that.

The idea that a male student can sexually harass a female professor . . . is insulting.

She has carried this first instance of sexual harassment around in her head for six years. It is the beginning of a long list. A serious feminist now, an inhabitant of the official feminist house on campus, she recognizes this experience for what it was. She knows there is no way to punish the anonymous offender or everyone would be behind bars, but she thinks the solution is education. Like many feminists, she argues that discipline is clumsy, bureaucracy lumbering, and there is no hope for perfect justice in the university. She is more concerned with getting the message across, delineating acceptable behaviors to faculty and students alike, than in beheading professors. She subscribes to a sort of zookeeper school of feminism—training the beasts to behave within "acceptable" parameters.

Many foreigners think that concern with sexual harassment is as American as baseball, New England Puritans, and apple pie. Many feminists in other countries look on our preoccupation with sexual harassment as another sign of the self-indulgence and repression in American society. Veronique Neiertz, France's secretary of state for women's rights, has said that in the United States "the slightest wink can be misinterpreted." Her ministry's commonsense advice to women who feel harassed by coworkers is to respond with "a good slap in the face."[14]

Once sexual harassment includes someone glancing down your shirt, the meaning of the phrase has been stretched beyond recognition. The rules about unwanted sexual attention begin to seem more like etiquette than rules. Of course it would be nicer if people didn't brush against other people in a way that makes them uncomfortable. It would also be nicer if bankers didn't bang their briefcases into people on the subway at rush hour. But not nice is a different thing than against the rules, or the law. It is a different thing than oppressing women. Etiquette and politics aren't synonyms.

Notes

1. "What You Should Know About Sexual Harassment." Princeton, N.J.: SHARE.

2. Ibid.

3. A standard definition given by a book about sexual harassment affirms that "harassment can also occur when no such formal [power] differential exists, if the behavior is unwanted by or offensive to the woman." Michele A. Paludi, ed., *Ivory Power: Sexual Harassment on Campus* (Albany: State University of New York Press, 1990), 38.

4. Catharine MacKinnon, *Feminism Unmodified* (Cambridge: Harvard University Press, 1987), 89.

5. *Chronicle of Higher Education*, 24 April 1991.

6. Billie Wright Dziech and Linda Weiner, *The Lecherous Professor: Sexual Harassment on Campus* (Chicago: University of Illinois Press, 1990), 180.

7. Sue Rosenberg Zalk, "Men in the Academy," in Paludi, 143.

8. Dziech and Weiner, 180.

9. Paludi, 122.

10. "Sexual Harassment: A Hidden Issue." Washington, D.C.: Project on the Status and Education of Women, 1978.

11. *Chronicle of Higher Education*, 10 July 1991.

12. "Due Process in Sexual Harassment Complaints," *Academe 77* (September-October 1991).

13. Dziech and Weiner, 49.

14. *New York Times*, 3 May 1992.

Organizations to Contact

The editors have compiled the following list of organizations concerned with the issues debated in this book. The descriptions are derived from materials provided by the organizations. All have publications or information available for interested readers. The list was compiled on the date of publication of the present volume; names, addresses, and phone numbers may change. Be aware that many organizations take several weeks or longer to respond to inquiries, so allow as much time as possible.

Center for Women's Policy Studies (CWPS)
2000 P St. NW, Suite 508
Washington, DC 20036
(202) 872-1770

CWPS is an independent feminist policy research and advocacy institution established in 1972. The center studies policies affecting the social, legal, health, and economic status of women. It publishes reports on a variety of topics related to women's equality and empowerment, including sexual harassment, campus rape, and violence against women.

Equal Employment Opportunity Commission (EEOC)
1801 L St. NW
Washington, DC 20507
(202) 663-4900

The purpose of the EEOC is to eliminate discrimination in the workplace. To achieve this purpose, the commission investigates cases of alleged discrimination, including cases of sexual harassment; helps victims prosecute cases; and offers educational programs for employers and community organizations. The EEOC publishes a packet of information about sexual harassment.

The Feminist Majority Foundation
1600 Wilson Blvd., Suite 801
Arlington, VA 22209
(703) 522-2214
hotline: (703) 522-2501

The foundation researches ways to empower women. It maintains a hotline that provides information, resources, and strategies for dealing with sexual harassment. The foundation publishes a report that includes an overview and critical analysis of sexual harassment laws and an examination of women's experiences of being sexually harassed. It also publishes the quarterly *Feminist Majority Report* as well as a newsletter, fact sheets, books, and videos.

Foundation for Economic Education (FEE)
39 S. Broadway
Irvington-on-Hudson, NY 10533
(914) 591-7230
fax: (914) 591-8910

FEE studies and promotes capitalism, free trade, and limited government. It occasionally publishes articles opposing government solutions to the problem of sexual harassment in its monthly magazine the *Freeman*.

The Heritage Foundation
214 Massachusetts Ave. NE
Washington, DC 20002
(202) 546-4400
fax: (202) 544-2260

The Heritage Foundation is a public policy research institute that advocates limited government and the free market system. It opposes affirmative action for women and minorities and believes that the private sector, not government, should be relied upon to ease social problems and improve the status of women. The foundation publishes the quarterly journal *Policy Review* as well as hundreds of monographs, books, and papers on public policy issues.

Men's Rights, Inc.
PO Box 163180
Sacramento, CA 95816
(916) 484-7333

Men's Rights, Inc., opposes feminism and believes that current antidiscrimination laws discriminate against men. It distributes articles on sexual harassment, including *A Case Against Society's Sexual Harassment of Men* and *Sexual Harassment . . . Again.*

National Coalition of Free Men
PO Box 129
Manhasset, NY 11030
(516) 482-6378

The coalition's members include men seeking a "fair and balanced perspective on gender issues." The organization promotes the legal rights of men in issues of abortion, divorce, false accusation of rape, sexual harassment, and sexual abuse. It conducts research, sponsors education programs, maintains a database on men's issues, and publishes the bimonthly *Transitions*.

National Organization for Women Legal Defense and Education Fund
99 Hudson St.
New York, NY 10013
(212) 925-6635

The fund provides legal referrals and conducts research on a broad range of issues concerning women and the law. It offers a comprehensive list of publications, including testimony on sexual harassment, books, articles, reports, and briefs.

The Rockford Institute
934 N. Main St.
Rockford, IL 61103-7061
(815) 964-5053

The institute promotes traditional male/female roles and family values. Among other topics, it studies issues related to women in the workplace, including sexual harassment. Publications include the monthly *Family in America, Religion and Society Report, Chronicles: A Magazine of American Culture,* and a quarterly newsletter, *Main Street Memorandum.*

Women's Legal Defense Fund
1875 Connecticut Ave. NW, Suite 710
Washington, DC 20009
(202) 986-2600
fax: (202) 986-2539

Founded in 1971, the Women's Legal Defense Fund is a national advocacy organization that works at the federal and state levels to develop and promote policies that help women achieve equal opportunity, quality health care, and economic security for themselves and their families. The fund advocates stricter legislation to reduce sexual harassment and other types of discrimination. It publishes fact sheets on sexual harassment.

Bibliography

Books

Titus E. Aaron with Judith A. Isaksen	*Sexual Harassment in the Workplace.* Jefferson, NC: McFarland & Co., 1993.
S.K. Biklen and D. Pollard, eds.	*Gender and Education.* Chicago: National Society for the Study of Education Yearbook, 1993.
E. Buchwald, P. Fletcher, and M. Roth, eds.	*Transforming a Rape Culture.* Minneapolis: Milkweed Editions, 1993.
Ellen Bravo and Ellen Cassedy	*The 9 to 5 Guide to Combating Sexual Harassment.* New York: John Wiley & Sons, 1992.
Billie Wright Dziech and Linda Weiner	*The Lecherous Professor: Sexual Harassment on Campus.* Champaign: University of Illinois Press, 1992.
Lynne Eisaguirre	*Sexual Harassment: A Reference Handbook.* Santa Barbara, CA: ABC-CLIO, 1993.
Martha J. Langelan	*Back Off! How to Confront and Stop Sexual Harassment and Harassers.* Washington: Sojourners Resource Center, 1994.
June Larkin	*Sexual Harassment: High School Girls Speak Out.* Toronto: Second Story Press, 1994.
Rush H. Limbaugh	*The Way Things Ought to Be.* New York: Pocket Books, 1992.
Barbara Lindemann and David D. Kadue	*Primer on Sexual Harassment.* Washington: The Bureau of National Affairs, 1992.
Catharine A. MacKinnon	*Feminism Unmodified: A Discourse on Life and Law.* Cambridge, MA: Harvard University Press, 1992.
Catharine A. MacKinnon	*Sexual Harassment of Working Women: A Case of Sex Discrimination.* New Haven: Yale University Press, 1979.
Jeffrey Minson	*Questions of Conduct: Sexual Harassment, Citizenship, Government.* New York: St. Martin's Press, 1993.
Celia Morris	*Bearing Witness: Sexual Harassment and Beyond: Everywoman's Story.* New York: Little, Brown, 1994.
Michele A. Paludi, ed.	*Ivory Power: Sexual Harassment on Campus.* Albany: State University of New York Press, 1990.
Michele A. Paludi, ed.	*Working 9 to 5: Women, Men, Sex and Power.* Albany: State University of New York Press, 1991.
Barbara Kate Repa and William Petrocelli	*Sexual Harassment on the Job.* Berkeley, CA: Nolo Press, 1992.
Robert O. Riggs, Patricia H. Murrell, and JoAnn C. Cutting	*Sexual Harassment in Higher Education.* Washington: George Washington University, 1993.

| Amber Coverdale Sunrall and Dena Taylor, eds. | *Sexual Harassment: Women Speak Out.* Freedom, CA: The Crossing Press, 1992. |
| Edmund Wall | *Sexual Harassment: Confrontations and Decisions.* Buffalo: Prometheus Books, 1993. |

Periodicals

Jerry Adler	"Must Boys Always Be Boys?" *Newsweek*, October 19, 1992.
Angela Bonavoglia	"The Sacred Secret," *Ms.*, March/April 1992.
Mona Charen	"Feminists Are Losing the Battle," *Conservative Chronicle*, April 13, 1994. Available from PO Box 11297, Des Moines, IA 50340-1297.
Jeffrey K. Clark	"Complications in Academia: Sexual Harassment and the Law," *SIECUS Report*, August/September 1993. Available from 130 W. 42nd St., Suite 2500, New York, NY 10036.
Suzanne Fields	"Battle of the Sexes Drifts into Dangerous Territory," *Insight*, July 5, 1993. Available from 3600 New York Ave. NE, Washington, DC 20002.
Suzanne Fields	"Is It Really Harassment?" *Insight*, December 9, 1992.
Anne B. Fisher	"Sexual Harassment: What to Do." *Fortune*, August 23, 1993.
Holly Gallagher	"Sexual Harassment: Prevention of Staff Victimization," *American Jails*, May/June 1994.
Miranda Van Gelder	"High School Lowdown," *Ms.*, March/April 1992.
Stephanie B. Goldberg	"Hostile Environments," *ABA Journal*, December 1991. Available from 750 N. Lake Shore Dr., Chicago, IL 60611.
Daniel Goleman	"Sexual Harassment: It's About Power, Not Lust," *The New York Times*, October 21, 1991.
William Norman Grigg	"A New Tool for Feminists," *The New American*, July 26, 1993.
Virginia R. Harris	"Hidden Harassment," *Crossroads*, April 1993.
Michele Ingrassia	"Abused and Confused," *Newsweek*, October 25, 1993.
Margaret A. Jacobs	"Riding Crop and Slurs: How Wall Street Dealt with a Sex-Bias Case," *The Wall Street Journal*, June 9, 1994.
Murray Kempton	"Sexual Harassment Knows Few Bounds in the 'Real World.'" *Liberal Opinion Week*, May 30, 1994. Available from PO Box 486, Vinton, IA 53249.
Lawrence Kutner	"Harmless Teasing or Sexual Harassment?" *The New York Times*, February 24, 1994.
Richard B. McKenzie	"The Thomas/Hill Hearings: A New Legal Harassment," *The Freeman*, January 1992. Available from the Foundation for Economic Education, Irvington-on-Hudson, NY 10533.
Naomi Munson	"Harassment Blues," *Commentary*, February 1992.

Susan P. Phillips and   "Sexual Harassment of Female Doctors by Patients," *The*
Margaret S. Schneider   *New England Journal of Medicine*, December 23, 1993.

Robert Reno   "Harassment Cases Need to Be on Firmer Ground,"
Liberal Opinion Week, May 23, 1994.

Jeffrey Rosen   "Reasonable Women," *The New Republic*, November 1,
1993.

Margery D. Rosen   "The Big Issue: Sexual Harassment," *Ladies Home Journal*,
September 1993.

Amy Saltzman   "It's Not Just Teasing," *U.S. News & World Report*, December 6, 1993.

Rochelle Sharp   "Capitol Hill's Worst Kept Secret: Sexual Harassment,"
Ms., January/February 1992.

Gail Silberman   "After *Harris*, More Questions on Harassment," *The Wall
Street Journal*, November 11, 1993.

Susan Brooks   "Sexual Harassment: To Protect, Empower," *Christianity
Thistlewaite   and Crisis*, October 21, 1991. Available from 537 W.
121st St., New York, NY 10027.

Cynthia Tucker   "Paying the Price of Sexual Harassment," *Liberal Opinion
Week*, May 23, 1994.

James M. Wall   "Political Trash Talk," *The Christian Century*, May 18-25,
1994.

James M. Wall   "What Is Sexual Harassment?" *The Christian Century*,
April 13, 1994.

Michael Weiss   "Crimes of the Head," *Reason*, January 1992.

Index

CAMBRIDGE
COMMUNITY LIBRARY.